ATTACKING
THE KING

ATTACKING THE KING

J. N. WALKER

OXFORD UNIVERSITY PRESS · 1976

Oxford University Press, Walton Street, Oxford OX2 6DP

OXFORD LONDON GLASGOW NEW YORK
TORONTO MELBOURNE WELLINGTON CAPE TOWN
IBADAN NAIROBI DAR ES SALAAM LUSAKA ADDIS ABABA
KUALA LUMPUR SINGAPORE JAKARTA HONG KONG TOKYO
DELHI BOMBAY CALCUTTA MADRAS KARACHI

Casebound ISBN 0 19 217556 4
Paperback ISBN 0 19 217557 2

© Oxford University Press 1976

Printed in Great Britain
by Fletcher & Son Ltd., Norwich

Acknowledgements

This book is dedicated to Bro. Alan, who found the path and lit the way.

Writing a book can be fun; it can also be hard work. In writing this follow-up to *Chess Openings for Juniors* I was fortunate in having much of the hard work taken from my shoulders, and I would like to thank most sincerely all those who have helped. Andrew Clark in particular card-indexed countless games at the research stage, while Steven Luckett and Mike Donaghay undertook the huge task of checking and rechecking the proofs. Christopher Sheehan and Andrew Cook both contributed en route, as did Heidi Falkous, whose help was particularly welcome, since she does not even play chess.

The diagrams were again prepared by Colin Hunter, who also found time to dig the garden whilst I got on with the writing—we both trust the book sales will prove more plentiful than the harvest!

The drawings are based on I.A. Sokolov's illustrations in Eugene Ilyin's splendid Russian fairy-tale book *The Adventurous Pawn*, and thanks are expressed to the Soviet Agency Fizkultura i Sport for permission to adapt and reproduce.

Oxford   *J. N. Walker*
July 1976

Contents

PART TWO: BUILDING A KING ATTACK

Notation

Throughout this book we use the long form of algebraic notation.

THE BOARD

Each row of squares across the board is called a *rank*, and is given a number starting from White's side.

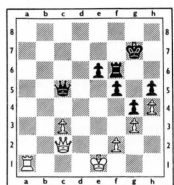

Each row of squares running up the board is called a *file*, and is given a letter starting from White's left hand side.

Each square is named by first giving the file letter and then the rank number. In our diagram the white rook stands at a1, the white queen at c2, the black king at g7, and so on.

THE SYMBOLS

We use symbols as abbreviations for pieces and chess terms.

K = king ♔   0-0 = castles on the K-side

Q = queen ♕   0-0-0 = castles on the Q-side

R = rook ♖   x = takes

B = bishop ♗   − = moves to

N = knight ♘   + = check (++ = double check)

The pawn (♙) has no symbol.   e.p. = en passant

We use ! to show a good move, and ? to show a bad move.

WRITING THE MOVES

There are four things to be written when recording a move.

(a) The symbol for the piece which moves (unless it is a pawn).

(b) The square it was standing on before moving.

(c) The action it makes.

(d) The square it moves to.

In the diagram opposite, the white rook which stands at a1 can move to a8 at the other end of the board. This would be written:

Ra1-a8

If check is given, the check sign is written after the move. In the diagram White can give check by playing his rook to a7:

Ra1-a7+

But then Black could capture the rook with his queen:

. . . Qc5xa7

As the pawn has no symbol the first of our four steps is left out when we write a pawn move. If White advances the pawn standing in front of his queen, the move is written:

c3-c4

NAMING PAWNS

A pawn is named after the file on which it stands. In the diagram, the pawn upon c3 is White's c-pawn (or queen's bishop's pawn). The pawn on e6 is Black's e-pawn (or king's pawn), and so on.

Some chess terms and expressions

RANK: a row of squares running across the board from left to right. The row from a1 to h1 is White's first rank.

FILE: a row of squares running from the white to the black side of the board. The a-file runs from a1 to a8; the b-file runs from b1 to b8, and so on. A pawn standing on a file belongs to that file; so the white pawn on a3 is the white a-pawn, and the black pawn on f7 is the black f-pawn.

K-SIDE: the half of the board to White's right: the e-, f-, g-, and h-files.

Q-SIDE: the other half of the board: the a-, b-, c-, and d-files.

OPEN FILE: a file on which neither side has a pawn. In the diagram the e-file and the h-file are both open.

HALF-OPEN FILE: a file upon which only one of the players has a pawn. In the diagram Black has two half-open files, the a-file and the d-file, while the c-file is half-open for White.

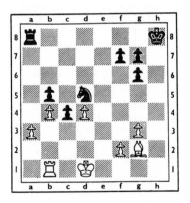

BLUNDER: a mistake.

DOUBLED PAWNS: when two pawns of the same colour are on the same file, they are said to be doubled. The black pawns on g7 and g6 are doubled on the g-file.

EN PRISE: a piece or pawn is said to be *en prise* when it is threatened. The black knight is *en prise* to the white bishop because Black has no way of recapturing if White plays Bg2xd5.

FIANCHETTO: a bishop is fianchettoed when the neighbouring knight's pawn has moved and the bishop is placed on its square. The white bishop on g2 is fianchettoed.

FLIGHT SQUARE: a square to which an attacked piece may run.

FORK: a double attack. If Black plays . . . Nd5-c3+ he is forking the white king and rook.

ISOLATED PAWN: a pawn is isolated when there is no pawn on the same colour on the files either side of it. The white pawn on d4 is isolated because there are no white pawns on the e-file or the c-file.

LOOSE: undefended.

MAJOR PIECES: queen and rooks.

MINOR PIECES: bishops and knights.

OPENING: the part of the game when the pieces are being developed. This leads to the MIDDLE-GAME, where the forces properly join battle. The ENDING or ENDGAME is reached when one side will need to queen a pawn in order to give checkmate.

PASSED PAWN: a pawn is passed when it can advance to the eighth rank to queen without being either blocked or taken by an enemy pawn. The white pawn on d4 and the black pawn on c4 are therefore both passed, but the white pawn on a3 is not.

PIN: a piece is pinned when it cannot move without exposing a more valuable piece to capture. In the diagram, the white bishop pins Black's knight onto his rook.

SACRIFICE: giving up a piece or a pawn in the hope of gaining some kind of advantage.

THE EXCHANGE: the advantage of a rook against a minor piece. If in the diagram 1 . . . Nd5-c7   2 Bg2xa8 Nc7xa8, Black has lost the exchange.

Beware the pointless check

'Never miss a check! it might be checkmate,' a famous international player once said.

Nonsense!

Check is not checkmate, and in chess it is checkmate that matters. Sometimes a check may help you on the way to checkmate, but a check may also be absolutely useless. Look at this example:

1	e2-e4	e7-e6
2	d2-d4	Bf8-b4+

The black bishop attacks the white king; it is check, but what has Black gained?

Nothing!

White will simply block the check with **3 c2-c3** and the miserable bishop will have to run away. The check was pointless, a total waste of time.

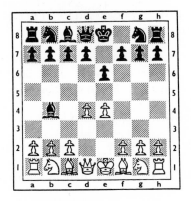

Make sure that you have a good reason when you check. Make sure that you are not just wasting time. *Don't just check for the sake of attacking the king.*

LOOK OUT FOR THE DEADLY QUIET MOVE

Often when you are attacking strongly and your opponent's king has come out into the open, you will find that you have several ways of giving check and driving your opponent's king around the board. Just as often you will find that a check is useless, and it is a quiet move that sets up the checkmate. Look at this diagram.

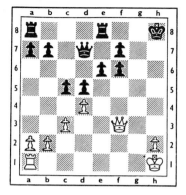

White to move

White is a rook down; he must look for checkmate. Let's see what happens if he plays the obvious check.

1	Qf3-h5+	Kh8-g8
2	Ra1-g1+	Kg8-f8
3	Qh5-h8+	Kf8-e7

White has just driven the black king to safety

Now let us see what happens if White plays a quiet move.

1 Ra1-g1! (*See Diagram*)

What can Black do?

Nothing!

He cannot stop 2 Qf3-h5 mate.

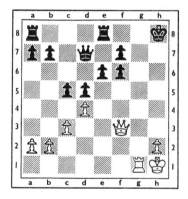

The quiet move set up the checkmate by trapping the black king against the side of the board, in a net from which he could not escape.

'Never miss a check; it might be checkmate.' Perhaps he meant that you should always consider every check. But, whenever you have the chance to check, always think hard. Will the check really annoy the king? Will it hurt your opponent? Will it help you towards checkmate?

Always remember that a check by itself is worth nothing. Check is only check. The king is only attacked. Check is not checkmate.

PART ONE

SEARCHING FOR CHECKMATE

1 The young lion

When the young Dutchman Max Euwe* took his place at a chess board in Amsterdam one afternoon in 1920, he didn't know that one day the chess world was to acclaim him its champion. He didn't know he was to become a Doctor of Philosophy, a Professor, a Grandmaster of chess, and the world's leading authority and writer on openings and chess theory. Max Euwe was eighteen, and, like you, no doubt he dreamed of such things. But, as he sat at the board, he didn't even know what fate held in store for him that very afternoon. He knew his opponent, though; Richard Réti had been playing international chess for some time, and a series of fine tournament triumphs in the previous two years had established him as one of the world's leading masters.

Max Euwe had the white pieces, and he was determined to have a go at the master, attack him hard, and try to capture a famous scalp.

Game 1
(*Two Knights Defence*)

Max Euwe	Richard Réti
1 e2-e4	e7-e5
2 Ng1-f3	Nb8-c6
3 Bf1-c4	Ng8-f6
4 d2-d4	

Euwe answers the Two Knights Defence with the Max Lange Attack, declaring his intention to fight a stormy battle.

4 ...   e5xd4

5 0-0

The pawn can be recaptured later: Euwe wants to bring his pieces rapidly into action.

5 ...   Nf6xe4

6 Rf1-e1   d7-d5

Réti defends his knight and strikes back in the centre.

7 Bc4xd5

Euwe continues the attack energetically; Black's centre is to be destroyed.

7 ...   Qd8xd5

8 Nb1-c3   Qd5-a5

9 Nf3xd4

*Say 'Urver'.

A very brave thrust! Euwe can see that after 9 Nc3xe4 Bc8-e6 he will have regained his piece but will leave Réti with an easy game. He boldly sacrifices a piece to gain a lead in development and open lines for his pieces to flow into the black position.

9 ...   Nc6xd4

10   Qd1xd4   f7-f5

Réti saves his knight with this move, because 11 f2-f3 would cost Euwe his queen to 11 . . . Bf8-c5.

11   Bc1-g5   Qa5-c5

12   Qd4-d8+   Ke8-f7

13   Nc3xe4   f5xe4

14   Ra1-d1

Now all Euwe's pieces are splendidly placed. He has a sizeable lead in development and is blasting away down the centre files with his heavy artillery. Réti is tied up, and he can't bring his pieces into play because both his bishops are pinned . . .

14 ...   Bf8-d6!

Already a piece ahead, Réti decides he can afford to hand back some material to ease his position.

15   Qd8xh8   Qc5xg5

16   f2-f4   Qg5-h4

Black does not take the pawn because (a) 16 . . . Qg5xf4   17 Re1-f1, and (b) 16 . . . Bd6xf4   17 Rd1-d8 both lose, while (c) 16 . . . e4xf3 e.p. allows White to bring his queen back into play with 17 Qh8-e8+.

17   Re1xe4

Euwe's heavy brigade continues to power down the middle, ripping into Réti's position. The master is still tied up, with his queen's bishop pinned . . .

17 ...   Bc8-h3!!

A superb move which kills Euwe stone dead!

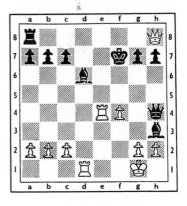

18   Qh8xa8

Otherwise his queen is lost.

18 . . . .   Bd6-c5+

19   Kg1-h1

Euwe cannot save himself by handing back a rook: 19 Re4-d4 Bc5xd4+ 20 Rd1xd4 Qh4-e1 mate.

19	...	Bh3xg2+!
20	Kh1xg2	Qh4-g4+
21	Kg2-f1	

Or 21 Kg2-h1 Qg4-f3 mate.

| 21 | ... | Qg4-f3+ |
| 22 | Kf1-e1 | Qf3-f2 mate |

Richard Réti was one point nearer winning first prize; Max Euwe was left with his hopes and his dreams.

Euwe had to wait fifteen years for his dreams about the world championship to come true. His immediate problem was to work out why he had lost to Réti. Euwe was not going to blame bad luck, or a stomach ache, or noisy spectators; he knew he had been beaten fair and square, and he was determined to find out why. He had chosen an aggressive opening and he had followed all the rules of opening play, developing quickly and keeping a careful eye on the centre. Then by sacrificing a piece he had seized the initiative, gained a lead in development, and brought all his pieces into play on splendid squares. His queen crashed down the middle breathing fire in all directions; his rooks gave powerful support from the rear. Réti's king was driven out into the open and his position tottered as first one rook and then the other fell to Euwe's queen. It all seemed simple and straightforward. Then in four more moves Euwe was lost. Dead and buried. And there had been nothing he could do about it.

On the chess board Euwe and Réti had played out a duel from the Roman arena. Euwe was the young lion, wild and ferocious. Réti was the gladiator, calm and professional. The lion had thrown himself upon his opponent, mauling savagely, intent only upon tearing him to pieces. The gladiator reeled under the onslaught, he watched, he waited, and when the opening appeared he struck swiftly with one sword thrust to the heart. The lion was dead; the gladiator, battered and bruised, lived to fight another day.

Euwe would not have taken long finding out why he had lost. There is only one aim in a game of chess: to checkmate the enemy king. Other smaller aims will crop up along the way; winning pieces; gaining advantages in development, space, and time; forcing the opponent to retreat his pieces to poor squares; and so on. But these are only ways of building up a big enough advantage to achieve the one aim of checkmate. Euwe had played his attack very well, it had been a successful attack, winning material. Unfortunately for Euwe, Réti's attack had also been a success, and was more important because it was aimed at the king. Euwe had been taught the lesson: CHECKMATE ENDS A GAME OF CHESS.

2   The value of pieces in battle

Bobby Blunder was going to be world champion one day. There was no
doubt about that, you only had to ask him! Unlike Max Euwe, Bobby
wasn't going to wait fifteen years for his dream to come true; Bobby
Blunder was in a hurry.

Mr Woodpusher came into the clubroom and headed straight for the
corner where he could see Bobby busily writing his thirtieth move on his
scoresheet. Bobby was playing the final game in the club tournament, and
needed to win to take first place. A quick glance at the board told Mr
Woodpusher that the game was almost over. Bobby's opponent, an elderly
gentleman, had lost almost all of his pieces and Bobby was getting ready
for the kill.

Bobby Blunder

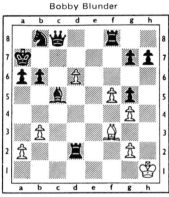

Elderly Gentleman to move

As soon as he saw his teacher Bobby got up.

'I'm winning it easily,' he said. 'He ought to resign; it's not sporting to
play on in such a hopeless position.'

'You be careful,' Mr Woodpusher told him. 'The game isn't over until
the last move has been made. You sit yourself down and think about what
you're doing; there will be plenty of time for talking after you've won.'

Bobby slouched back in his seat. There were times, he thought, when
Mr Woodpusher seemed to have little faith in him. The elderly gentleman
puffed on his pipe and stared at the board. Time slowly passed. Bobby
yawned, gazed vacantly around the room, fiddled with his pen, and tried
to look thoroughly bored. The elderly gentleman wasn't a bit put out; he
just puffed on his pipe and carried on thinking. At length he stirred, stopped
puffing and thinking, and moved:

31   d6-d7

'At last!' thought Bobby. 'I've only got to get my rook onto the h-file and it's checkmate. If I move my rook to f6 now, he can take my queen with his pawn and get a queen back himself . . . but that doesn't matter because I can then put my rook on h6 and it's checkmate! . . . in fact it doesn't matter what he does . . . he can't stop me mating him . . . besides, it'll look good to sacrifice my queen . . .'

31   . . .   Rf8-f6

Bobby wasn't bored any more; he was going to checkmate next move. The elderly gentleman looked puzzled.

'Poor old chap,' Bobby thought, 'he's done his best. The cup will look good at home . . . we'll keep it in the living room . . . on top of the television would be a good place . . . Mum will keep it clean . . . and she can show it off to all the visitors . . . Mr Woodpusher will be pleased as well . . . he's been a great help, but I wish he'd have more faith in me . . . sometimes he seems to think I'm stupid . . . what shall I spend the prize money on? . . . I think I'll . . .'

32   d7xc8=N

Bobby was rudely awoken from his dreams as his opponent smiled and held out his hand.

'I'm very sorry, but that seems to be checkmate,' the elderly gentleman said apologetically, clambering to his feet. 'Bad luck young man, a pity after you had played so well!'

Bobby stared blankly at the position in front of him. He was stunned. Everything had blown up in his face. His queen sacrifice. His checkmate. The game. The tournament. All that he had worked so hard to achieve throughout the season. Everything had been wasted, all because of one silly move and that wretched white knight. He slumped back in his seat, peered up at Mr Woodpusher through watery eyes, and felt suddenly rather sick.

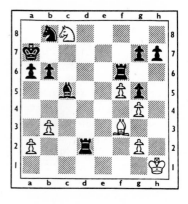

There was much that Mr Woodpusher wanted to say, but this was not the time or the place to say it; Bobby had had quite enough for one evening. Even so there was one point he had to make right now. He smiled kindly at Bobby, slowly shook his head, and sat down opposite the youngster.

'Chess is like boxing,' he said. 'A boxer can knock his opponent all round the ring for half an hour, leaving him bruised and bleeding, and still get caught by one silly punch. Then he finds himself flat on his back, unable to get up, and all the good work he has done earlier counts for nothing. Chess is just the same. It doesn't matter how easily you seem to be winning; as long as your opponent has one little pawn left he can still beat you. A chess game is usually lost by the player who makes the last important mistake. It doesn't matter how well you have played for the first 30 moves, it doesn't matter how much better than your opponent you have proved yourself to be; if you make a silly mistake on move 31 then you have had it. At all times, even when the position is very simple, you must concentrate, think hard, and make absolutely certain. Never be in a hurry; always check that your king is safe; and remember that a game is never over before the last move has been made. Until then you can still lose.'

Next day Mr Woodpusher was in fine form, and Bobby, somewhat recovered, was keen to listen.

'I'll show you a game,' the teacher said. 'It's a very old and well-known game, played by a German chap called Anderssen. It was played in London, in 1851 I think it was, and begins with a wild King's Gambit, which was very popular in those days. Anyway, don't worry too much about the opening. Look at the game and see what you can learn about the value of the pieces in battle.'

Game 2

(King's Bishop's Gambit)

A. Anderssen	L. Kieseritzky
1 e2-e4	e7-e5
2 f2-f4	e5xf4
3 Bf1-c4	Qd8-h4+

He shouldn't be attacking so soon in the opening. 3 . . . d7-d5 would have been much better, giving back the pawn to gain freedom for his pieces, so that he could get on with the important job of development.

4 Ke1-f1   b7-b5
He doesn't like White's bishop aiming at f7; so he lures it away.

5	Bc4xb5	Ng8-f6

At last he gets on with his development, but with this move he blocks his queen's line of retreat.

6   Ng1-f3
Sensible development with gain of time.

6   . . .   Qh4-h6

7   d2-d3   Nf6-h5
This threatens to win the exchange with 8 . . . Nh5-g3+, but he is still attacking when he should be developing his pieces.

8   Nf3-h4   Qh6-g5

9   Nh4-f5   c7-c6

10 g2-g4   Nh5-f6
Once again Kieseritzky has allowed his queen to be shut out!

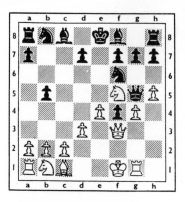

Now Anderssen threatens 15 Bc1xf4, winning the black queen, and Kieseritzky must do something about it.

14 . . .   Nf6-g8

15 Bc1xf4   Qg5-f6

16 Nb1-c3
White's pieces are racing out onto good squares.

16 . . .   Bf8-c5

17 Nc3-d5!   Qf6xb2

11 Rh1-g1!
Anderssen boldly sacrifices his bishop in order to get a lead in development.

11 . . .   c6xb5

12 h2-h4   Qg5-g6

13 h4-h5   Qg6-g5

14 Qd1-f3

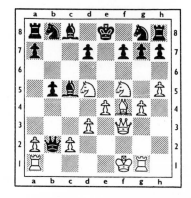

Kieseritzky is now on the receiving end of a rather nasty shock, for Anderssen sacrifices both rooks.

18 Bf4-d6!! Qb2xa1+

19 Kf1-e2 Bc5xg1

He can't very well capture the rook with his queen, since she is needed to defend g7: 19 . . . Qa1xg1 20 Nf5xg7+ Ke8-d8 21 Bd6-c7 mate.

20 e4-e5

White closes the queen's diagonal and again threatens to capture on g7 and mate on c7.

20 . . . Nb8-a6

Black defends the mating square.

21 Nf5xg7+ Ke8-d8

22 Qf3-f6+!!

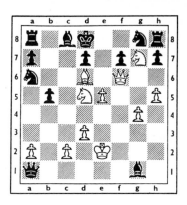

The final master stroke.

22 . . . Ng8xf6

23 Bd6-e7 mate

'Well, what do you think?'

'That was brilliant,' Bobby's face was wide with wonder.

'Yes, it was,' Mr Woodpusher continued. 'But what did you learn about the value of the pieces?'

'Well . . .,' Bobby frowned and thought for a moment. 'Black won a lot of pieces; in fact he had a queen, two rooks, and a bishop more at the end . . . but they weren't worth much to him because they couldn't stop the checkmate. White only had three pieces, but they all helped checkmate Black's king . . . so I suppose they were worth more, but . . .'

'Exactly!' Mr Woodpusher interrupted. 'The bigger army is not always the stronger army. Anderssen gave up a lot of pieces so that the few he had left could checkmate his opponent's king. You must remember that it is checkmate that matters, not the number of pieces you have left at the end of the game. You must always be on the look out for the possibility of giving up pieces, sacrificing them to get at the enemy king.'

THE POWER OF THE SACRIFICE IN THE KING ATTACK

We can immediately lay down one rule: *if you can trap the enemy king it doesn't matter how many pieces you give up; if you get a checkmate then their sacrifice is worthwhile.*

Obviously you can't just go around sacrificing pieces willy nilly, tossing them away for nothing but some vague hope that you might be lucky enough to find a mate. You must have a very good reason for sacrificing anything. Sacrifices can:

(a) Gain time to attack.

(b) Drive or drag defending pieces away from the king.

(c) Rip open the pawns protecting the king so that your pieces can get at him.

Almost every sacrifice in successful attacks on the king has one of these three ideas. If we look at Anderssen's sacrifices we can see how each has one of these ideas behind it. Look at the position after move 10:

Position after 10 . . . Nh5-f6

Both players have two pieces in play. On move 11 White sacrifices his bishop, and Black's next four moves are forced.

11	Rh1-g1	c6xb5
12	h2-h4	Qg5-g6
13	h4-h5	Qg6-g5
14	Qd1-f3	Nf6-g8
15	Bc1xf4	Qg5-f6
16	Nb1-c3	

Now White has five pieces in active play to Black's one. By sacrificing his bishop White has gained an enormous amount of time, and his pieces are ready to start the attack on the black king.

(16 . . . Bf8-c5   17 Nc3-d5! Qf6xb2)

Next Anderssen sacrificed the rooks:

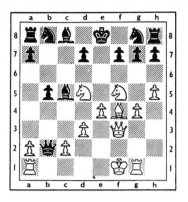

Position after 17 . . . Qf6xb2

18	Bf4-d6	Qb2xa1+
19	Kf1-e2	Bc5xg1
20	e4-e5	

White has given up two rooks, but has gained the two moves Black has wasted making the captures. Black's two active pieces have been dragged up the board, and are out of play, unable to defend their king.

(20 . . . Nb8-a6 21 Nf5xg7+ Ke8-d8)

Finally Anderssen gave up his queen:

Position after 21 . . . Ke8-d8

Kieseritzky's knights are desperately defending the black squares. White plays:

22 Qf3-f6+

Now the black knight on g8 is overloaded; he wants to remain on g8 to defend the mate threat on e7, but he is dragged away because he has to capture the white queen:

(22 . . . Ng8xf6 23 Bd6-e7 mate)

Anderssen's sacrifices illustrate the first two ideas very clearly. Look at Game 3 and you will see the same ideas again; only this time Black finishes the game off with a sacrifice that illustrates our third idea of ripping apart the king's position.

Game 3
(Giuoco Piano)

1	e2-e4	e7-e5
2	Ng1-f3	Nb8-c6
3	Bf1-c4	Bf8-c5
4	d2-d3	Ng8-f6
5	Bc1-g5	d7-d6
6	0-0	

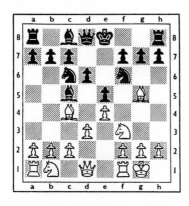

White puts his king into what looks like a safe corner. Black, however, has not yet castled, and gets the chance to advance on the K-side, and gain time by attacking White's pieces.

6	. . .	h7-h6
7	Bg5-h4	g7-g5
8	Bh4-g3	h6-h5!

Black begins sacrificing pawns. His immediate aim is to remove the knight and bishop which are doing defensive duty around White's king, and at the same time break open the files for his own attack.

| 9 | Nf3xg5 | |

The knight begins its travels, and Black gains time for the advance of his h-pawn.

| 9 | . . . | h5-h4 |

More material is offered, and the knight wanders further from home.

| 10 | Ng5xf7 | |

| 10 | . . . | h4xg3! |

Black throws his queen into the melting pot. In exchange he gains time for his attack, and removes the bishop which defends the white king.

| 11 | Nf7xd8 | Bc8-g4 |

White's queen is attacked. He cannot play f2-f3; nor can he make the capture f2xg3, because of the black bishop raking the diagonal from c5 onto his king.

| 12 | Qd1-e1 | Nc6-d4 |

Now the threat is 13 . . . Nd4-e2+ 14 Kg1-h1 Rh8xh2 mate.

| 13 | Nb1-c3 | |

White defends e2 but Black produces a sacrifice which illustrates our third idea.

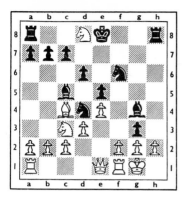

13 ...   Nd4-f3+!
The shield of pawns in front of the white king is ripped apart, so that Black's rook and bishop can get at the king.

14   g2xf3
The alternative 14 Kg1-h1 Rh8xh2 is mate.

14   ...   Bg4xf3
Now Black threatens 15 ... g3xh2 mate, and White can't escape with 15 h2xg3, because of Rh8-h1 mate.

15   h2-h4   Rh8xh4

16   White resigns

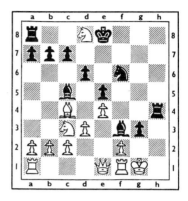

White has no way of stopping 16 ... Rh4-h1 mate.

Notice how all the sacrifices fit into our pattern. The white knight is lured away from the defence of the king, and wastes time capturing the pawns on g5 and f7, and the queen on d8. Black uses the time he gains to bring his active pieces into threatening positions. Then, when everything is prepared, he springs his last sacrifice, opens up the white king, and delivers the final blow.

A sacrifice does not always have to end in checkmate. Sometimes the threat of mate is enough to force your opponent to give up more pieces to save his king than you have sacrificed to attack it. Then you are left with a winning advantage. Game 4 shows Black sacrificing and White having to give up pieces to avoid being mated.

Game 4
(Scotch Game)

1	e2-e4	e7-e5
2	Ng1-f3	Nb8-c6
3	d2-d4	e5xd4
4	Nf3xd4	Ng8-f6
5	Nd4xc6	b7xc6
6	Bf1-d3	d7-d5

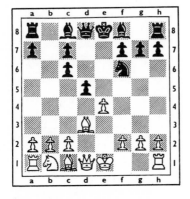

Black secures an equal game by fighting for the centre. White normally plays 7 e4xd5 in this position, but here he lets fly at the black knight.

7	e4-e5	Nf6-g4
8	0-0	Bf8-c5

The pawn on e5 could not be taken at once (if 8 . . . Ng4xe5 9 Rf1-e1 and 10 f2-f4), so Black develops and pins the white f-pawn against the king.

9	h2-h3	Ng4xe5!

White probably thought that Black could not afford this capture, but Black is prepared to give up the knight so that he can gain time for his attack.

10	Rf1-e1	Qd8-f6
11	Qd1-e2	

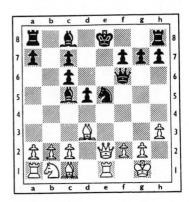

The black knight is lost, since 11 . . . Bc5-d6 is met by 12 f2-f4.

11	. . .	0-0

A fine sacrifice which tempts the white queen away from the defence of f2.

12	Qe2xe5	Qf6xf2+
13	Kg1-h1	

If the king had gone to h2, then 13 . . . Bc5-d6 would have cost White his queen.

13	. . .	Bc8xh3!

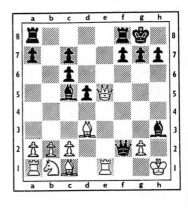

A second fine sacrifice; Black offers the bishop to smash away the defences around the enemy king.

14   g2xh3
If 14 Bd3-f1, . . . Qf2-g1 is mate.

14   ...   Qf2-f3+
Now the white king is exposed, Black must strike quickly before White finds time to gather his defenders. With only two pieces in play he cannot force mate, but he can win White's queen.

15   Kh1-h2   Bc5-d6

16   Qe5xd6
White is forced to give up material.

16   ...   Qf3-f2+
Cunning! 16 . . . c7xd6 would have left Black only a little ahead, but this way he wins a rook as well.

17   Kh2-h1   Qf2xe1+

18   Kh1-g2   c7xd6

19   White resigns

Black has a big lead in material, the white king is still exposed, and there is no way for White to get back into the game.

Although this game didn't end in checkmate, Black's two piece sacrifices were successful because they followed our three aims. In the king attack sacrifices should:

(a) Gain time.

(b) Remove defenders.

(c) Open up the king.

BEWARE! WHEN YOU SACRIFICE THERE IS NO TURNING BACK

Pieces are valuable; you must be sure when you sacrifice that you are going to get enough in return. If you don't, then you have simply lost material. Look at Game 5. White sacrifices merrily, but can he catch the black king?

Game 5
(*Latvian Gambit* or *Greco Counter Gambit*)

1	e2-e4	e7-e5	5	. . .	Qg5xg2
2	Ng1-f3	f7-f5	6	Qd1-h5+	g7-g6
3	Bf1-c4		7	Bc4-f7+	Ke8-d8

White meets the gambit with straightforward development. The black king is rather exposed; it may be possible to catch him before he can find safety, if White can bring his pieces into action quickly enough.

3	. . .	f5xe4
4	Nf3xe5	Qd8-g5

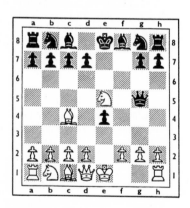

Faced with the threat of 5 Ne5-f7, Black decides to counter-attack.

5   d2-d4

The white queen wants to join the battle with check at h5, but first the black queen must be driven out of the way, and the knight must be protected.

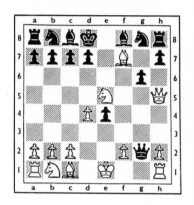

White has reached the moment of great decision! He can exchange queens by 8 Qh5-g5+; then he has a small lead in development as compensation for being a pawn down. But, if he wants more, White must be prepared to sacrifice.

8   Bf7xg6

White accepts the challenge; he offers a rook and a bishop to pull the black queen further out of play and to gain time for the attack.

8	. . .	Qg2xh1+
9	Ke1-e2	Qh1xc1
10	Ne5-f7+	Kd8-e8

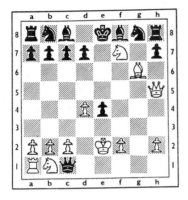

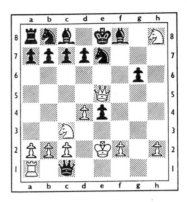

Black survives the first test; 10 . . . Kd8-e7 would have allowed 11 Qh5-e5 mate. Now White has another problem; he has a confusingly large number of good-looking moves: Nf7xh8+, Nf7-d6++, Nf7-e5+, Qh5-e5+, Bg6xe4, or he can bring his queen's knight into the attack and offer his other rook. Which move is best?

11 Qh5-e5+

A rook and a bishop behind, has White found the right answer? Can he catch the black king?

11 . . .   Ng8-e7

12 Nf7xh8+   h7xg6

13 Nb1-c3

With only a queen and a knight in action, White does not have enough fire power for his attack. Although he is two pieces behind he offers the second rook to bring the other knight into play.

13 . . .   Qc1xc2+

14 Ke2-e1

The best square. On f1 the white king would have to face an eventual . . . Bc8-h3+, and if 14 Ke2-e3 Black wins at once by 14 . . . Bf8-h6+.

14 . . .   Qc2xb2

15 Nc3xe4

An evil plot is being hatched! White threatens 16 Ne4-f6+ Ke8-d8 17 Nh8-f7 mate.

15 . . .   Qb2xa1+

16 Ke1-e2   Qa1xa2+

Foiled! Black clings on by the skin of his teeth; his queen controls f7 and stops the mate.

19	Kf3xg4	d6xe5
20	Ne4-f6+	Ke8-d8
21	Nh8-f7+	Kd8-c8
22	**White resigns**	

17 Ke2-f3   d7-d6

At last Black has found breathing space for his king.

18 d4-d5

Two bishops and a rook behind, White tries one last desperate fling. He offers his queen to cut off Black's defence of f7. Now if 18 ... d6xe5 19 Ne4-f6+ Ke8-d8 20 Nh8-f7+ is mate all over again.

18 ...   Bc8-g4+

Foiled again! Black finds the solution; he makes more room for his king.

At last the black king has found a safe home. White has run out of checks, and Black has the massive advantage of a queen, a rook, a bishop, and two pawns.

White's sacrifices followed our ideas. The black queen was dragged up the board and she wasted time on her journey; White used this time to bring his pieces to fighting stations. The attack began with White firing all the shots and the black king struggling to survive. Yet survive he did; and White slowly ran out of ammunition. Finally the attack ground to a halt. White had nothing left to throw at the black king, and Black had his large army waiting to take over. White lost because he gave up so many pieces that he just had to find a checkmate. Hard though he tried he couldn't mate the black king, and his opponent wriggled out. Then Black won simply because he had more pieces.

When you sacrifice you must remember that every chess piece has two totally different values:

(a) The *General Value* is the obvious value. A queen is worth more than a rook because she is more powerful: she can do more. A rook is worth more than a bishop, and so on.

(b) The *Immediate Value* is much less obvious; it is based on what the piece can do in the actual position in the game.

The difference between these values will become clear if we look at Game 6.

Game 6
(*Vienna Game*)

1	e2-e4	e7-e5
2	Nb1-c3	Bf8-c5
3	Nc3-a4	Bc5xf2+!?

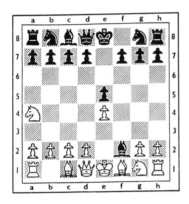

Black solves the problem of what to do about his bishop in a dramatic way. The aim of the sacrifice is to rip open the white king's position so that the black queen can get at him.

4	Ke1xf2	Qd8-h4+
5	Kf2-e3	

He cannot very well put the pawn in the way; 5 g2-g3 Qh4xe4 leaves him with his rook to defend and his knight stranded on a4.

5	...	Qh4-f4+
6	Ke3-d3	d7-d5
7	Kd3-c3	

White decides that life is too hot for his king in the centre, so he sets out to look for safety on the Q-side. Since he is a piece ahead White knows that he should win if he can

keep his king out of danger, and not fall too far behind in development.

7	...	Qf4xe4
8	Kc3-b3	Nb8-a6
9	a2-a3	

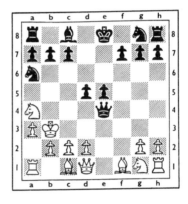

No doubt White feels happy at this point. He has just beaten off the threat of 9 . . . Qe4-b4 mate, and at the same time he has made a nice hole for his king on a2. Alas! he is in for a shock.

9	...	Qe4xa4+

An astonishing sacrifice! Black now draws his opponent's king up the board and tries to catch him in a mating net.

10	Kb3xa4	Na6-c5+
11	Ka4-b4	a7-a5+!

Yet another sacrifice. Black is long past the point of no return. He has no hope of regaining a queen; so he must lose unless he can trap the white king. The flames of his attack must be kept alive, and the knight is just more fuel to keep the fire burning.

12   Kb4xc5   Ng8-e7

Very clever! Black seems to be simply defending his pawn on d5. In fact he is threatening to play 13 . . . b7-b6+   14 Kc5-b5 Bc8-d7 mate. Poor White can't find a safe place for his king, and his reply is forced.

13   Bf1-b5+   Ke8-d8

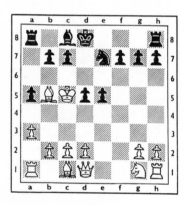

Now 14 . . . b7-b6 would be mate; so White must move his bishop again.

14   Bb5-c6   b7-b6+

15   Kc5-b5   Ne7xc6

The white king is never left in peace. The threat this time is 16 . . . Nc6-d4+ 17 Kb5-a4 Bc8-d7 mate. How White must wish he could retreat his king to safety; then he would be able to win easily with his extra pieces. But the king must go forward.

16   Kb5xc6   Bc8-b7+!

Yet more fuel for the fire. Black is a queen and knight behind; so an extra bishop won't hurt.

17   Kc6-b5

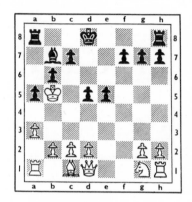

White correctly realizes he can't afford 17 Kc6xb7 Kd8-d7   18 Qd1-g4+ Kd7-d6, since he has run out of checks and can't stop 19 . . . Rh8-b8 mate.

17   . . .   Bb7-a6+

18   Kb5-c6

Once again White would dearly love to retreat his king to safety. However, after 18 Kb5-a4 Ba6-c4 there would be no way of preventing 19 . . . b6-b5 mate.

18   . . .   Ba6-b7+

19   Kc6-b5   Bb7-a6+

20   Kb5-c6   Ba6-b7+

21   Kc6-b5

(See Diagram Above)

Here the game was given up as a draw, since both sides are just moving the same pieces backwards and forwards, repeating the position. White would win if he could stop Black from checking him, but he can't. Black would win if he could find a checkmate, but there isn't one to be found!

Now we see the difference between the two values of the pieces; the *general value* and the *immediate value*. The general value of White's pieces is large; he has a queen and knight more. The immediate value of White's pieces is small because they are all undeveloped and can do absolutely nothing to help their king avoid the checks.

The general value of Black's pieces is small (he has only two pawns in exchange for White's queen and knight), but their immediate value is tremendous! The black bishop is giving the annoying checks, and if he is ever captured then the rooks will join forces to give mate.

This difference of value is the important point to remember when sacrificing. Pieces are valuable, they are not like confetti to be chucked around at a wedding. When you give up a piece the general value of your army goes down, and you will lose unless you can do something immediately.

Once you have sacrificed there is no turning back. Victory will go to the larger army unless you can strike immediately.

SOMETHING IS BETTER THAN NOTHING

Black saved himself from defeat in the last game even though he was more than a queen behind and could not find a mate. Although he had no hope of winning, Black was able to draw, and this is much better than losing. There are two ways in which a player who is hopelessly behind in material can try to save the game by a draw: *perpetual check*, and *stalemate by attacking the king*.

PERPETUAL CHECK

This was the way Black escaped in the last game. The game ended in a draw because White could not stop his opponent's checks. Here is another example:

Game 7
(Ruy López)

1	e2-e4	e7-e5
2	Ng1-f3	Nb8-c6
3	Bf1-b5	a7-a6
4	Bb5-a4	Ng8-f6
5	0-0	Nf6xe4

Black has chosen the fighting Open Defence, and hopes to get free play for his pieces.

6 d2-d4   e5xd4
This capture is risky. Black opens the e-file, and leaves his knight in danger.

7	Rf1-e1

White is quick to seize his chance.

7	...	d7-d5
8	Nf3xd4	

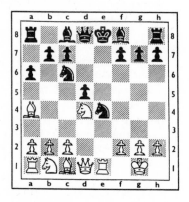

Now Black seems to be in real trouble; White threatens both 9 f2-f3 winning the knight, and 9 Nd4xc6 b7xc6 10 Ba4xc6+ winning the exchange.

8	...	Bf8-d6
9	Nd4xc6	Bd6xh2+!

Black makes a desperate effort to save himself.

10	Kg1xh2	Qd8-h4+
11	Kh2-g1	Qh4xf2+
12	Kg1-h1	Qf2-h4+
13	Kh1-g1	Qh4-f2+

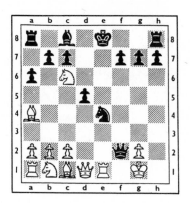

Once again White cannot avoid the checks, and Black, two pieces behind, escapes with a draw. In Game 7 Black sacrificed to destroy the white king's defences; in Game 8 Black catches the king undefended in the centre:

Game 8
(*Grünfeld Defence*)

1	d2-d4	Ng8-f6
2	c2-c4	g7-g6
3	Nb1-c3	d7-d5
4	Bc1-f4	Bf8-g7
5	e2-e3	c7-c5

With his bishop on the long diagonal from h8 to a1, Black aims to fight for the black squares in the centre.

6	d4xc5	Qd8-a5
7	c4xd5	Nf6xd5!

Neat! But has Black seen far enough?

8	Qd1xd5	Bg7xc3+
9	b2xc3	Qa5xc3+
10	Ke1-e2	Qc3xa1
11	Bf4-e5	

No; it would seem Black has gone wrong.

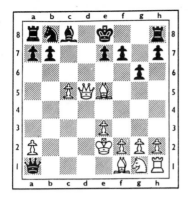

15 Kf3-e2

He can't risk 15 Kf3-g3 Qf5-g4 mate!

15	...	Qf5-c2+
16	Ke2-e1	Qc2-c1+

11	...	Qa1-c1
12	Be5xh8	Bc8-e6
13	Qd5xb7	Qc1-c2+

Yes! Black has calculated correctly after all. White cannot avoid the checks.

14	Ke2-f3	Qc2-f5+

And a draw is forced by perpetual check. White can't get his king away, and Black, a piece and pawn down, cannot hope for more.

STALEMATE BY ATTACKING THE KING

This can happen only when there are very few pieces left on the board. If you are badly behind in material and hope to escape in this way, your king must be in a stalemate position. Look at the diagram below. White is three pawns down; his king is in a stalemate position; but he still has a rook which he can move.

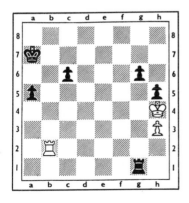

White finds a brilliant way to set up a stalemate position. He plays:

1 Rb2-b7+!

Now Black is stuck. If he captures the rook, then White can't move, and it is stalemate. So Black moves:

1 ... Ka7-a8

and White simply checks again:

2 Rb7-b8+!

The game is drawn. Black cannot get his king away from the checks, and if
he ever takes the rook, then White has a draw by stalemate. Here the black
king was trapped against the side of the board, but it would have made no
difference if he could have wandered everywhere. Look at the next example.

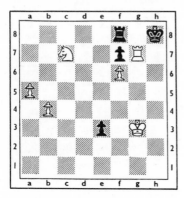

Black to move

Black is in deep trouble, a piece and
pawn behind. But he finds a clever
way out:

1	...	e3-e2
2	Kg3-f2	

The pawn must be stopped.

2	...	e2-e1=Q+
3	Kf2xe1	Rf8-e8+!

And the rook cannot be taken
since Black will be in stalemate.

4	Ke1-f2	Re8-e2+
5	Kf2-g3	Re2-g2+
6	Kg3-f4	Rg2-f2+

Not 6 . . . Rg2-g4+, which allows
7 Rg7xg4, breaking the stalemate
position.

7	Kf4-e4	Rf2-f4+

And wherever the king goes, the
rook goes as well! He can never be
taken without stalemate.

The chance of stalemate does not occur very often, but perpetual check
frequently crops up in games where there has been a king attack. One side
has sacrificed to open up the enemy king, he cannot find a mate, but he can
keep checking. In this way he gets half a point from the game. Be on the
look-out for the chance of perpetual check when you are attacking the
king, or when your own king is being attacked. Remember, half a point is
something, and it is much better than nothing!

WINNING IS IMPORTANT. PLAY TO WIN, NOT TO BE CLEVER

Bobby Blunder had done it again! Mr Woodpusher glared at him across the board; his face twisted into a look which Bobby recognized only too well, a look which said 'You poor fool', and 'You make me want to scream', both at the same time! Bobby didn't need Mr Woodpusher to tell him, he knew himself that he should have won.

The game had started well; Bobby, as Black, defended the Queen's Gambit, won a piece with an opening trap, got on with his development, and seemed set for any easy win. Then he had tried to be clever . . .

Game 9
(Queen's Gambit)

1	d2-d4	d7-d5
2	c2-c4	e7-e6
3	Nb1-c3	Ng8-f6
4	Bc1-g5	Nb8-d7
5	Ng1-f3	c7-c6
6	e2-e3	Qd8-a5

Bobby plays the lively Cambridge Springs Defence, and his opponent makes the natural developing move which turns out to be a mistake.

7	Bf1-d3	Nf6-e4
8	Nf3-d2?	

White gives away a piece.

8	. . .	Ne4xd2

Bobby could take the bishop straight away, with 8 . . . Nc4xg5, but he wants to bring his queen over for a K-side attack.

9	Qd1xd2	d5xc4
10	Bd3xc4	Qa5xg5

Now Bobby has won a piece; his opponent has no compensation; and winning should be simple.

11	0-0	b7-b5
12	Bc4-d3	Bf8-d6
13	Ra1-d1	0-0
14	Rf1-e1	Nd7-f6

Bobby groups his pieces for the final attack on White's king.

15	e3-e4	

White opens the diagonal from queen to queen, and threatens 16 e4-e5 regaining his piece. The exchange of queens is the simple answer for Bobby, but he has set his heart on a king attack, and suddenly a clever idea forms in his mind.

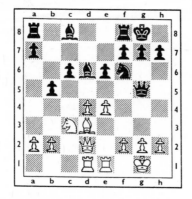

| 15 | ... | Qg5-h5!? |
| 16 | e4-e5 | Bd6-c7 |

The first point of Bobby's plan: if the knight is captured, he can get at the white king.

17	e5xf6	Qh5xh2+
18	Kg1-f1	Qh2-h1+
19	Kf1-e2	Qh1xg2

The second point, and this is where Bobby has been really clever: White can't prevent ... e6-e5, and then Bobby plans ... Bc8-g4+ and ... Qg2-f3 mate. A brilliant combination, and he'd worked it all out on move 15!

20 Re1-g1
Only now does Bobby begin to realize what is going to happen.

21	...	Qg2-h3
22	Rg1xg7+	Kg8-h8
23	Rg7xh7+	Qh3xh7
24	Bd3xh7	Kh8xh7
25	Qd2-g5	Black resigns

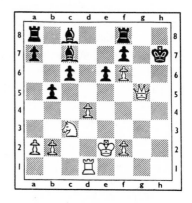

White threatens mate by either Rd1-h1 or Qg5-g7.

Bobby sat uneasily, waiting for Mr Woodpusher to explode. He knew very well that he should have won; he knew very well that by losing he had cost his side the match. He was also reasonably certain that Mr Woodpusher was not exactly pleased.

'I was unlucky,' Bobby suddenly blurted out. He didn't really believe that himself, and one glance was enough to show that Mr Woodpusher was not convinced either.

'Oh yes?' came the reply.

'Well . . . it would have been brilliant . . . if it had worked.'

'But it didn't work, did it?'

'No.' Bobby began to feel rather sorry for himself. (He seemed to be spending far too much time feeling sorry for himself these days.) There was a lengthy pause.

'Never mind, it was a good try,' Mr Woodpusher smiled, and Bobby felt a little brighter. 'I was pleased to see you using your imagination, and then having the courage to sacrifice and carry out your plan. Let's look at that position, and see what we can learn.'

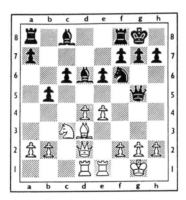

Position after 15 e3-e4

'You are a piece ahead, and your opponent has no compensation; so you are winning. In every position where you are material ahead you should follow a simple four point plan:

(a) Exchange as many pieces as possible.

(b) Use your extra piece in the ending to attack and win enemy pawns.

(c) Queen one of your own pawns.

(d) Checkmate the enemy king with your new queen.

The value of pieces in battle

When you are winning there is no reason at all for taking chances. By exchanging pieces you make your opponent's army weaker, and the weaker it becomes, the less chance there is of his getting back into the game.'

'So I should have played 15 . . . Qg5xd2, exchanging queens.'

'Correct,' Mr Woodpusher went on. 'Then your opponent's most powerful piece has been removed from the board, and it becomes almost impossible for him to build an attack against your king. Of course, you have to forget your own plans for a king attack, but that doesn't matter, because you have an extra piece and will win the ending.'

Mr Woodpusher set up the pieces again. 'You weren't the only one,' he said. 'Look at this.'

Bobby soon guessed that this was the game from the bottom board; it had been played by two very young boys, and Bobby was amused by some of the silly mistakes.

Game 10
(Centre Game)

1	e2-e4	e7-e5
2	d2-d4	Nb8-c6
3	Bf1-b5	Nc6xd4
4	Qd1-h5	g7-g6?

Bobby was right; it wasn't a very good game.

5	Qh5xe5+	Bf8-e7
6	Qe5xh8	Be7-f6
7	Qh8xg8+	Ke8-e7

'Right,' said Mr Woodpusher. 'What should White do now?'

'That's easy,' Bobby replied. 'Exchange queens.'

'Of course, but just look what actually happened.'

8	Qg8xh7	Nd4xc2+
9	Ke1-f1	d7-d5
10	e4xd5	Qd8xd5
11	Bb5-a4?	Qd5-d1 mate

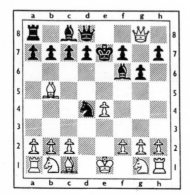
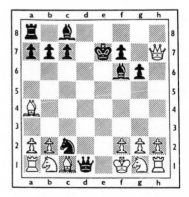

'What a dreadful game . . .' Bobby began.

Mr Woodpusher cut him short before he could say any more. 'Yes, just like your game, wasn't it?'

Bobby flushed.

'Instead of exchanging queens and winning simply and easily with a rook and a knight more in the endgame, White kept his attack alive by keeping the queens on the board. O.K., he was still winning, and he had to make a very silly mistake to lose, but if White had done the simple thing and exchanged queens, there would have been no way for Black to get a quick mate with his few remaining pieces.

'You must remember that the one aim in chess is to checkmate your opponent; it doesn't matter how, and it doesn't matter when. You don't get an extra point for being clever, nor for being quick. When your attack has won a piece, you should play simply for the ending. Don't take chances by following a doubtful attack, and never try to be clever. You are winning anyway, so don't take risks.'

SUMMARY

Pieces are important. Without an army you cannot win any battle. In chess, victory will normally go to the larger army; so you will lose if you give pieces away for nothing. Yet there will often be positions where a few well-placed pieces can defeat a large chess army. In these positions you can sacrifice because what you get in return (checkmate perhaps) is worth more than what you have given up. You must be very careful though; make sure that your attack really is getting somewhere, and if you find you have gone wrong look for a way out with a perpetual check. If your attack fizzles out, then you have sacrificed for nothing, and you will soon find that your opponent's larger army is going to win the game for him.

Finally, just as you will realize that you are losing when you fall a piece behind, so you must realize that you are winning when you have a similar advantage. Having got a winning advantage you must never give your opponent a chance to get back into the game. Play simple chess, exchange pieces, and queen a pawn in the ending.

Pieces are valuable; look after them!

3 Fire-power – the road to checkmate

Young David chose a stone, whirled his sling, and let fly. Goliath, ten feet of Philistine giant, toppled and crumpled in a heap. David stepped forward, took the giant's sword, and chopped off his head. Magnificent! Triumph for the weak over the strong.

Unfortunately this sort of thing doesn't happen very often. If you are faced with an enemy twice your size, you know very well what will happen. Unless you are clever enough and quick enough to run like mad in the opposite direction, you will soon join Goliath, spreadeagled on your back!

In chess there is nowhere to run; you have to stand and fight. If the enemy pieces facing your king are stronger, have greater fire-power, than your defenders, then they will be able to batter their way through and get at your king. Look at Game 11 and see the fire-power White puts into his attack:

Game 11
(Queen's Gambit Declined)

1	d2-d4	d7-d5
2	c2-c4	Ng8-f6
3	c4xd5	Nf6xd5
4	e2-e4	Nd5-f6
5	Nb1-c3	e7-e6
6	Ng1-f3	Bf8-b4
7	Bf1-d3	Nb8-c6
8	Bd3-c2	0-0
9	Qd1-d3	

White's pieces begin to take up menacing positions; the queen and bishop are striking hard along the diagonal from b1 to the heart of the enemy king position. Immediately White is threatening to attack Black's knight by 10 e4-e5, and if the knight moves White will play 11 Qd3xh7 mate.

9	...	g7-g6

Black blocks the diagonal.

10	a2-a3	Bb4xc3+
11	b2xc3	Rf8-e8
12	e4-e5	

A fine blow; driving the black knight away from f6, its best defensive square.

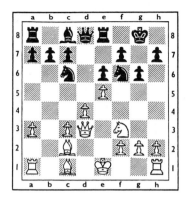

The concentrated fire-power of White's pieces is terrific, and Black is overwhelmed. Just look at the number of pieces White has queueing up to pour into Black's king position: a queen, a rook, two bishops, and a knight. And what has Black to offer in defence? Only a pair of pawns; he will need a move or two to bring any other piece to the defence. With such a large advantage in strength White will quickly batter his way through.

12 ...   Nf6-d7

13 h2-h4!

White already has his queen and bishops raking the diagonals leading to Black's king; now he wants to open the h-file so that his rook can join the attack.

13 ...   b7-b6

Black's position is in a dreadful state! The white army is massing its forces and Black has only a flimsy row of pawns ready to face the onslaught.

14 h4-h5   Bc8-b7

15 h5xg6   f7xg6

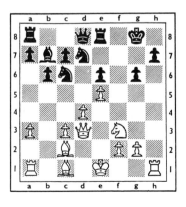

16 Rh1xh7!

The rook cannot be captured by 16 ... Kg8xh7, because 17 Qd3xg6+ Kh7-h8 18 Qg6-h7 is mate.

16 ...   Nd7-f8

The knight drops back to defend against the immediate threat of 17 Qd3xg6+, but what can one knight do against all White's attacking pieces?

17 Rh7-h6

Now the threat is 18 Rh6xg6+ Nf8xg6 19 Qd3xg6+ Kg8-f8 20 Bc1-h6+ Kf8-e7 21 Qg6-g7 mate. Black brings his other knight over to help cover g6, but his defenders are still overpowered.

17 ...   Nc6-e7

18 Nf3-g5

The knight joins the attack and the black queen is in trouble. Black now has to face the threat of 19 Rh6-h8+ Kg8-g7 20 Rh8xf8, when he cannot recapture because of 21 Ng5xe6+. Capturing the rook is no better: 19 ... Kg8xh8 20 Ng5-f7+.

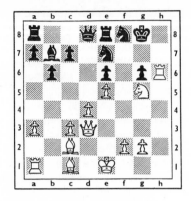

18 ... **Qd8-d5**

19 Qd3-h3

The final attack is to come along the h-file. Black's problem is that whilst the strength of White's attacking forces steadily increases, he is un-

able to bring any of his own major pieces to the defence of his king.

19	...	**Ne7-f5**
20	**Bc2xf5**	**e6xf5**
21	**Rh6-h8+**	**Kg8-g7**
22	**Qh3-h6 mate**	

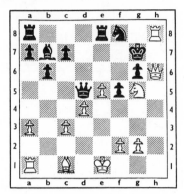

White's attack crashed through by sheer weight of numbers. White had so many pieces itching to attack, and Black had so few in position to defend, that from the moment White pushed his pawn to e5 the result was never in doubt.

Both sides began the game with the same number of pieces, and the same number of pawns. The two armies were absolutely equal as they faced each other across the board. Why then did White's pieces become so much more powerful? Why was White able to direct so much fire-power at the black king? The answer to these questions is that White had open files and diagonals for his pieces. When the line on which one of your pieces is standing becomes open, the power of the piece increases.

PIECES NEED OPEN LINES TO SHOW THEIR FULL FIRE-POWER

In Game 12 White once again clears the diagonals and files leading to Black's castled position. The white pieces come into active play and travel by express down the open lines. Black collapses under the fire-power of White's pieces.

Game 12
(King's Gambit)

1	e2-e4	e7-e5
2	f2-f4	e5xf4
3	Ng1-f3	Ng8-f6
4	e4-e5	Nf6-h5
5	Qd1-e2	Bf8-e7
6	d2-d4	0-0
7	Nb1-c3	d7-d6

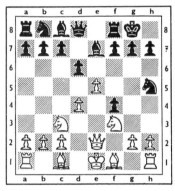

Black wants to exchange pawns to open lines for his pieces, but it is White who is able to bring his pieces into action first.

8	Bc1-d2	d6xe5
9	d4xe5	Be7-h4+

This is the point of Black's play; he seems to be catching the white king in the centre. However, White finds a neat sacrifice, opening lines on the K-side, and quickly turns the tables.

10	g2-g3!	f4xg3

11	0-0-0	Bc8-d7

Black blocks the open d-file, where White's rook is already looking dangerous.

12	h2xg3	Nh5xg3
13	Qe2-h2	Ng3xh1
14	Nf3xh4	

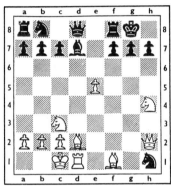

Let's stop and study this position for a minute. Black has a material advantage, and his king is castled safely behind the pawn shield. But is the king really safe? The rook and queen may be able to offer some help to their king, but the other black pieces are too far away to be of any use. On the other hand every one of White's pieces is well placed to join in a K-side attack, and the open files and diagonals are there, leading to the black king, just waiting for the white pieces to use them.

White's plan is clear; he must sort out his rather scattered pieces into an organized fighting force. If he can do this successfully, he will have far too much fire-power for the black defenders.

14 ...   Bd7-g4

15 Bf1-d3!

White can cheerfully sacrifice his rook to seize the open diagonal for his bishop. With a queen, two bishops, and a knight in attack, he has enough fire-power to mate two black kings!

15 ...   Bg4xd1

16 Nh4-f5

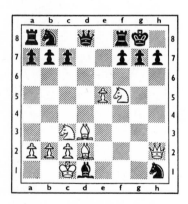

White's once ramshackle army has now taken up a fine attacking formation, and Black is hopelessly outgunned. The half-open h-file and the diagonal from d3 to h7 are the main lines of attack, and White is immediately threatening mate in two by 17 Nf5-e7+ and 18 Qh2xh7.

16 ...   g7-g6

The only real alternative for Black is to give up his queen by 16 ... Qd8xd3, but then White has a material advantage to go with his attack.

17 Qh2-h6

Threatening mate on g7.

17 ...   g6xf5

18 Bd3xf5

Again threatening mate; this time on h7.

18 ...   Rf8-e8

19 Bf5xh7+   Kg8-h8

20 Bh7-g6+   Kh8-g8

21 Qh6-h7+   Kg8-f8

22 Qh7xf7 mate

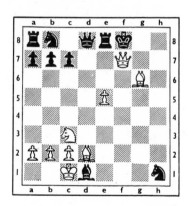

There were four steps in White's winning plan:

(a) He opened lines.

(b) He grabbed the h-file for his queen.

(c) He seized the diagonal from d3-h7 for his bishop.

(d) He smashed through by outnumbering the black defenders.

Open lines and greater fire-power go hand in hand. Look at Game 13 for another example. Black's pieces get the open lines this time, and they sweep across the board at White's castled position.

Game 13
(Ruy López—Marshall Gambit)

1	e2-e4	e7-e5	9	e4xd5	Nf6xd5
2	Ng1-f3	Nb8-c6	10	Nf3xe5	Nc6xe5
3	Bf1-b5	a7-a6	11	Re1xe5	Bc8-b7
4	Bb5-a4	Ng8-f6			
5	0-0	Bf8-e7			
6	Rf1-e1	b7-b5			
7	Ba4-b3	0-0			
8	c2-c3	d7-d5			

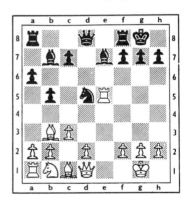

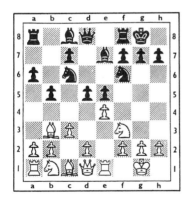

With this move Black sacrifices his e-pawn. In return for the pawn he gets open lines for his pieces, and the chance to attack.

Normally Black plays 11 . . . c7-c6 in this position, but in this game he plans to attack White along the diagonal from b7 to g2.

12   Re5-e1?
White hastily retreats his rook. He would have done better with 12 d2-d4, planning to answer 12 . . . Be7-d6 with 13 Re5xd5.

12	. . .	Be7-d6
13	d2-d4	Qd8-h4

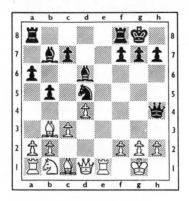

Black's plan is beginning to work; his queen and bishops command the important diagonals and sweep powerfully towards the white king ... and where are the white defenders?

14 g2-g3

White blocks the diagonal leading to h2, and cuts down the fire-power of Black's bishop on d6. However, Black's other bishop on b7 becomes even stronger.

14 ...   Qh4-h3

Now the power of the bishop on b7 becomes clear. Black threatens 15 ... Nd5-e3 followed by ... Qh3-g2 mate.

15 Qd1-f3

White tries to counter on the important long diagonal, but it is Black who has the greater fire-power on the K-side.

15 ...   Ra8-e8

The rook gives more fire-power as Black switches the attack to the open e-file, threatening mate on White's first rank.

16 Bc1-e3

Black has two lines of attack; the long diagonal and the e-file. White closes the file, and gets killed on the diagonal!

16 ...   Nd5xe3

Now we can see that it is the black bishop and not the white queen which controls the long diagonal. If 17 Qf3xb7 Ne3-g4 and Black mates.

17 Bb3xf7+

White grabs at a final straw, but sinks all the same.

17 ...   Rf8xf7

18 Qf3xb7

Now 18 ... Ne3-g4 is met by 19 Re1xe8+, but with *all* his pieces attacking the K-side, Black has too much fire-power for the white defenders.

18 ...   Rf7xf2!

Threatening mate in one on h2, and mate in two on f1.

| 19 | Kg1xf2 | Qh3xh2+ |
| 20 | Kf2-f3 | Qh2-g2 mate |

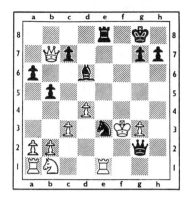

A neat and amusing finish. Just when the white queen seems to have taken command of the long diagonal, the black queen bursts in through the back door!

Again there was a four-point plan behind Black's victory.

(a) He opened lines for his pieces.

(b) He occupied the long diagonal with his bishop.

(c) He thundered along the open e-file with his rook.

(d) He powered his way through by outnumbering the white defenders.

Games 11, 12, and 13 should all have made it pretty clear that if the power of the attacking pieces greatly outweighs that of those defending, the attacker will be able to batter his way through by strength alone. It should also be clear that attacking pieces are strongest when they are mobile, when they have open files and diagonals, when they have room to move around.

Look at Game 14. White doesn't throw many pieces into his attack, and Black seems to have more than enough defenders. But White grabs an enormous advantage in space, and the black pieces become cramped and get in each other's way. White suddenly finds that his pieces can flash across the board and rip open Black's king position.

Game 14
(King's Gambit Declined)

1	e2-e4	e7-e5
2	f2-f4	Nb8-c6
3	Ng1-f3	d7-d6
4	Bf1-c4	Ng8-h6?

This is a silly square for the knight, and later on Black has to waste time moving it again.

| 5 | 0-0 | Bf8-e7 |

| 6 | d2-d3 | 0-0 |
| 7 | f4-f5 | |

As they advance they leave space behind them, and White's pieces become more powerful.

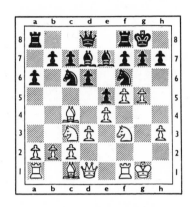

With this simple pawn move White seizes an advantage in space; he shuts in Black's light-squared bishop, and opens a fine dark diagonal for himself. The white bishop threatens immediately to zoom the full length of the diagonal, capture the black knight (8 Bc1xh6 g7xh6), and shatter Black's pawn shield.

| 7 | ... | Nh6-g4 |
| 8 | Nb1-c3 | |

If Black wants to win back some of the space he has lost, then he must try to play . . . d6-d5 soon. White develops and hammers hard at d5, making it difficult for Black to advance his pawn.

8	...	Bc8-d7
9	h2-h3	Ng4-f6
10	g2-g4	a7-a6
11	g4-g5	

The K-side pawns are on the march.

| 11 | ... | Nf6-e8 |
| 12 | h3-h4 | Kg8-h8 |

Black is worried about the bishop on c4; he unpins his f-pawn, but allows his king to be trapped in the corner.

13 Nf3-h2

White clears the diagonal for his queen to join the attack.

| 13 | ... | f7-f6 |
| 14 | g5-g6 | h7-h6 |

All of Black's pieces are defensively placed, but they are hopelessly cramped, shut into the centre with no room to move around, and they cannot help their king.

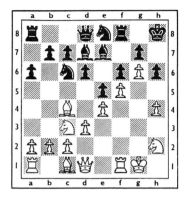

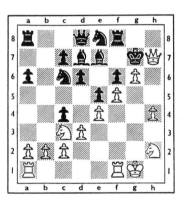

The important white pieces are the queen and the two bishops. See how White's advantage in space has given them open diagonals; highways to the black king. White seizes his chance.

15 Qd1-h5
The queen streaks across the open diagonal with a powerful threat: 16 Bc1xh6 g7xh6 17 Qh5xh6 mate.

15 ... b7-b5
Black stabs at the bishop which cuts off the king's retreat.

16 Bc1xh6!
A fine move! White ignores the threat to one bishop and sends the other into battle, charging along the open diagonal and crashing into Black's pawn shield. White's queen and bishops provide tremendous fire-power; Black cannot sort out his tangled pieces to defend his king.

16 ... b5xc4
17 Bh6xg7++ Kh8xg7
18 Qh5-h7 mate

White's invasion force was made up of a queen, two bishops, and a pawn; both bishops were sacrificed and mate was executed by the queen and the pawn alone. All the time Black's whole army of defenders was huddled together nearby, unable to give any help to the king. When he advanced his pawns White gained a large advantage in space on the K-side. The black pieces became cramped, and got in each other's way, because there were no open files or diagonals for them to use. The white pieces found freedom, gained enormous fire-power, and scythed apart Black's defences along the open diagonals.

Space gave White open lines, increased the fire-power of his pieces. Lack of space lowered Black's fire-power, and in the end it cost him the game.

What have we found out so far?

(a) If an attacking force has a large advantage in fire-power, it must be able to batter its way into the enemy position.

(b) The fire-power of a piece increases when it gets an open line to work along.

(c) Open lines and freedom of movement result from an advantage in space.

The only question left to be answered is: How do we get an advantage in space?

SPACE AND OPEN LINES WILL APPEAR WHEN YOU CONTROL THE CENTRE

In Game 15 White tries to set up a pawn centre; Black misses his chance to hit back, and White gets control in the middle of the board.

Game 15
(Giuoco Piano)

1	e2-e4	e7-e5
2	Ng1-f3	Nb8-c6
3	.Bf1-c4	Bf8-c5
4	c2-c3	

White wants to set up his centre pawns on d4 and e4, opening the diagonals for his bishops, and giving freedom to all his pieces.

4	...	Ng8-f6
5	d2-d4	e5xd4
6	c3xd4	Bc5-b4+
7	Nb1-c3	

Now Black should play 7 ... Nf6xe4, and then ... d7-d5 as soon as possible. In this way he would gain a foothold in the centre.

7	...	0-0?
8	d4-d5	

The white pawns begin their march forward, sweeping aside the black knights, and leaving oceans of space in their wake.

8 ...   Nc6-e7

If he plays 8 . . . Nc6-a5, then after 9 Bc4-d3 his knight is trapped on the edge of the board.

9   e4-e5   Nf6-e4

10   Qd1-c2

White protects his own knight, attacks the black one, and lets loose his queen on the diagonal to h7.

10   ...   Ne4xc3

11   b2xc3   Bb4-c5

White's centre pawns have captured an enormous amount of space, and they stand guard over Black's position ready to counter any break-out.

12   Nf3-g5

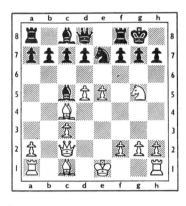

Even though he hasn't finished developing White starts his attack. He can only do this because he has such an advantage in space that his undeveloped pieces have files, and diagonals ready and waiting.

12   ...   Ne7-g6

Black stops the mate threat, but he is horribly cramped, and will have

trouble bringing any more pieces over to help his king.

13   h2-h4

The attack goes into full swing. White threatens to kick the black knight out of g6, so that he can mate on h7: 14 h4-h5 Ng6-e7   15 Qc2xh7 mate.

13   ...   h7-h6

14   d5-d6!

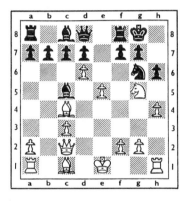

The hungry pawn gobbles up more ground and opens the line of action for White's king's bishop. Black's f-pawn is now pinned; so White's queen has gained more fire-power and threatens 15 Qc2xg6.

14   ...   h6xg5

15   h4xg5

The black knight can't run away, so White is in no hurry to regain his piece. Opening the h-file so that his rook can blast down its full length is far more important than material. With the rook in action White has enough fire-power to catch the black king.

15	...	Rf8-e8
16	Qc2xg6	Re8xe5+
17	Ke1-f1	Qd8-e8

Now Black has an open line and threatens mate at e1, but it is just too late.

18	Qg6-h7+	Kg8-f8
19	Qh7-h8 mate	

The black queen and rook got into play only when the game was all over. Like Black's other pieces they had neither the time nor the room to get to the scene of battle, around their king. This was because White's pawns won space in the centre, and his pieces took total control of that space. Then it was easy; the white pieces gained fire-power from the space and finished off the black king.

Game 16 is another example; White's pieces win control of the centre, and then switch over for a K-side attack.

Game 16
(*Sicilian Defence—Dragon Variation*)

1	e2-e4	c7-c5
2	Ng1-f3	Nb8-c6
3	d2-d4	c5xd4
4	Nf3xd4	Ng8-f6
5	Nb1-c3	g7-g6
6	Bc1-e3	Bf8-g7
7	Bf1-e2	0-0
8	0-0	d7-d6
9	f2-f4	Nf6-g4

Black hopes that he can exchange a few pieces and weaken White's attacking chances. In particular he wants to get rid of one of White's bishops, but in doing so he will lose his own king's knight, which should be doing the important job of defending his K-side and attacking the centre.

10 Be2xg4   Bg7xd4?

This is a dreadful move. Black exchanges the one piece he has actively defending his king position, a piece which also attacks the black squares in the centre.

11 Be3xd4   Bc8xg4

12 Qd1-d2

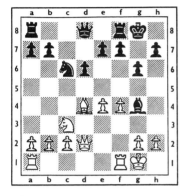

Black would have preferred
12 Qd1xg4 Nc6xd4, but White has no intention of allowing his queen to be drawn out of the centre.

12 . . .   Bg4-e6

13 f4-f5   Be6-c4

14 Rf1-f3   Nc6xd4

It is easy to understand that Black wants to remove White's dangerous bishop, but in doing so he exchanges the only piece he had left fighting for the centre.

15 Qd2xd4   Bc4-a6

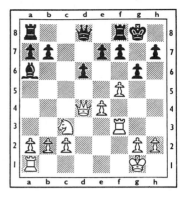

White's central control is complete. Not one black piece threatens the centre, whilst White's queen and knight dominate the position. This gives White the advantage in space, and we can already see the lines of attack open for his rooks, and the freedom he has to switch his pieces around the board, in any direction.

16 Nc3-d5!

White begins the final assault. The black king is defended by little more than the flimsy line of pawns; if White can bring his pieces to bear on the K-side, then he must have the fire-power to destroy the black king's position.

16 . . .   Ra8-c8

17 f5-f6   Rc8-c4

18 Qd4-d2

The white queen has been driven from her powerful post, but such is White's advantage in space that she immediately finds another good diagonal.

Fire-power—the road to checkmate

18	...	e7xf6

19 Qd2-h6

Threatening mate in two by
20 Nd5xf6+ Kg8-h8 21 Qh6xh7.
Black now closes one line of attack,
but White has too much fire-power
to be held off for long.

19	...	f6-f5

20 Rf3-h3   Black resigns

Black is mated after 20 . . . Rf8-e8
21 Qh6xh7 Kg8-f8 22 Qh7-h8.

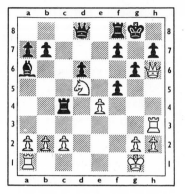

With a queen, a rook, and a knight knocking at his front door, it is not
surprising that the black king was caught so quickly. In this game Black
simply committed suicide! When he exchanged the minor pieces he made
two errors of judgment. One, he left himself without a hope of challeng-
ing the centre, and White had soon taken total control with his knight
entrenched on d5 and his queen breathing fire in all directions from d4.
This central control gave White increased fire-power. Two, Black weakened
his own fire-power on the K-side, and had absolutely nothing with which
to meet White's invasion force.

At the start of the game you must have two main ideas in mind. You
must try to develop rapidly to bring your pieces into play in good fighting positions, and you must try to control the centre. When you control
the centre you gain an advantage in space. Your pieces gain freedom; they
can be easily switched from one side of the board to the other; their fire-
power increases.

SUMMARY

Question   What are you trying to do in a game of chess?

Answer   Checkmate the enemy king.

Question   Which piece will the enemy defend most carefully?

Answer   His king.

Conclusion   The enemy king is likely to be well guarded, so it will be the most difficult target for you to attack.

You must not expect to be able just to develop a few pieces and then set off in pursuit of your opponent's king. A king attack takes great care and planning, and cannot be successful if the conditions are not right for attack. Your pieces are a fighting army. They can attack properly only if they are in the right place at the right time, if they have room to move around, if they can work together and support each other, if the reserve forces can quickly be brought up to the front line.

Chess is a battle, and like most battles it is won by the side with the greater fire-power. There is a three-rung ladder for you to climb:

(1) Try to control the centre and gain an advantage in space. Your pieces will be most powerful when they have room to move freely around the board.

(2) Seize good open files and diagonals for your pieces. These will be the lines of attack, freeways into your opponent's position.

(3) Attack when you see that the fire-power of your pieces is far greater than that of the enemy defenders. Then you can pound away at the enemy fortress, and keep on pounding until the walls fall down about his king.

You must try to be Goliath. David may seem brave and dashing, but it is Goliath who usually wins!

4 Snap mates – executing the prisoner king

We have just spent a whole chapter studying the way the powerful massacre the weak, the way the big always seem to triumph over the small. How then, did David manage to kill Goliath?

David won because of the simple fact that one well-aimed shot can sometimes be just as effective as a whole barrage of blows. Goliath towered above him, proud, strong, and above all confident, absolutely certain he would cut David to pieces. Goliath laughed at the boy, the Philistine army laughed and jeered. Goliath took out his sword, stepped forward, smiled, and decided exactly which part of David to carve off first . . . then, David hit him!

Let us turn this back into chess terms. Normally checkmate is achieved by one side powerfully building up an attack and surrounding the enemy king. Yet sometimes a checkmate arrives completely out of the blue, a total surprise to a player who had not thought he was in any danger at all. If we look back to Bobby Blunder's game with the elderly gentleman, we can see why poor unsuspecting Bobby was struck by a thunderbolt from the sky:

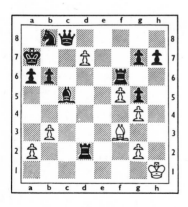

White to move

Black is many pieces ahead and winning comfortably. The white king is trapped, a prisoner in the corner, and checkmate cannot be far away.

But what about the black king? Where can he move to? Nowhere! Immediately an alarm bell should have gone off in Bobby's mind!

White wasn't going to miss his chance. He thought to himself, 'The black king can't move anywhere, so how can I check him? A check might well be mate!' Then the elderly gentleman had another think and found the right move: **32 d7xc8=N mate.**

There should have been no surprise that the black king was mated; all White had to do was check him! Giving check needs only one piece, not a whole army. Just as David killed Goliath with one sling shot, so the elderly gentleman finished off Bobby's king with a snap mate. Usually a snap mate catches a player by surprise only because he didn't realize that there was any danger; he was too sure of himself.

You will always make mistakes. You will rarely see everything that is going on in a position, and there are bound to be times when your king suddenly falls to a snap mate. However, there is one point which will help you.

WHENEVER YOUR KING IS IMPRISONED, LOOK OUT FOR A SNAP MATE

We can see a king that has few places to run in this diagram.

White to move

The black king has only two safe squares, c7 and b6. White needs a check on the diagonal from a5, and finds the move **1 Bg5-d8 mate.**

The next example is a little more complicated.

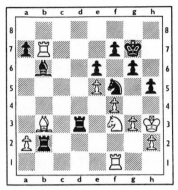

Black to move

White looks to be doing quite well. He threatens both Bb3xe6 and Nf3-g5, and his own king seems quite safe, protected by the pawn chain, a rook, and a knight. However, things do not quite work out the way White is expecting. Black notices that the white king, far from being safe, has nowhere to run.

The square h2 is a keg of dynamite, and the white king is sitting on it!

1 ...   Rd3xf3!
A fine sacrifice, knocking out White's best defensive piece.

2 Rf1xf3
After this White is mated; but if he doesn't recapture then he is a knight down.

2 ...   Bb6-g1
Black lights the fuse . . .

3 g3-g4   Rb2xh2 mate
. . . and blows the king sky high.

Black noticed how his knight and h-pawn were imprisoning the white king, and he looked for a snap mate. He was lucky!

We have looked at two positions where a king has run short of space and been trapped. Now we will see how the chance of trapping a king can arise in a game.

Game 17
(*Ruy López*)

1	e2-e4	e7-e5
2	Ng1-f3	Nb8-c6
3	Bf1-b5	Nc6-d4

Bird's Defence; an old-fashioned method of play.

4	Nf3xd4	e5xd4
5	Bb5-c4	

This wastes a move; White would have done better to castle.

5	...	Ng8-f6
6	e4-e5	d7-d5

Black is already striking out for freedom in the centre.

7	Bc4-b3	Bc8-g4
8	f2-f3	Nf6-e4!

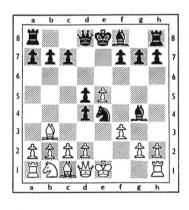

9 0-0

And not 9 f3xg4 Qd8-h4+ 10 g2-g3 Ne4xg3, when Black stands very well. White chooses to put his king into safety on the K-side. But it soon becomes apparent that the K-side is not as safe as he would have hoped!

9	...	d4-d3!

A really excellent little move which ties White up completely. The diagonal is opened onto the white king, and White's own development is held up because he can't move his d-pawn.

10	f3xg4	Bf8-c5+
11	Kg1-h1	

The white king has been shunted off into a corner.

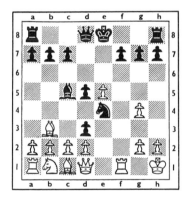

Now Black prepares to snap shut the trap.

11	...	Ne4-g3+
12	h2xg3	

Forced.

12	...	Qd8-g5

The white king's corner has become a death cell, and there is no escape. All Black has to do is arrange the execution; already he is threatening 13 . . . Qg5-h6 mate.

13　Rf1-f5

The only way of delaying the end.
Now 13 . . . Qg5-h6+ is answered
by 14 Rf5-h5.

13　. . .　　　h7-h5!!

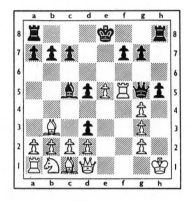

Black tries to open the h-file so
that his rook can get at the white
king.

14　g4xh5

Again White beats off the mate
threat. Black just can't get the check
he needs on the h-file: 14 . . . Rh8x
h5+　15 Qd1xh5 Qg5xh5+　16 Rf5
xh5 wins for White.

14　. . .　　　Qg5xf5

Black has to settle for the white
rook; but now he is threatening
again to capture on h5.

15　g3-g4　　　Rh8xh5+!

Black continues the attack energetically; White must not be given the
chance to play g2-g3, when his king
might wriggle out of the trap.

16　g4xh5　　　Qf5-e4

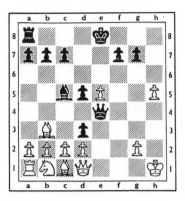

The white g-pawn is pinned, and
White is threatened with mate on h4.

17　Qd1-f3　　　Qe4-h4+

18　Qf3-h3　　　Qh4-e1+

Now the white king is neatly tied
up in his corner and mated.

19　Kh1-h2　　　Bc5-g1+

20　Kh2-h1　　　Bg1-f2+

21　Kh1-h2　　　Qe1-g1 mate

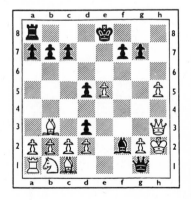

The black bishop on c5, shutting the king in the corner, was the key to the king's death cell. In Game 18 the white king becomes similarly trapped on the Q-side.

Game 18
(Centre Game)

1	e2-e4	e7-e5
2	d2-d4	e5xd4
3	Qd1xd4	Nb8-c6
4	Qd4-e3	g7-g6
5	Bc1-d2	Bf8-g7
6	Nb1-c3	Ng8-e7

9	e4xd5	Nc6-b4

The pawn on d5 can be recaptured later; first Black wants to get on with improving the position of his pieces.

10	Bf1-c4	Bc8-f5

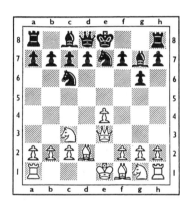

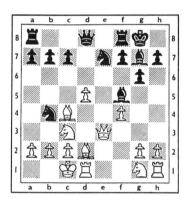

7 0-0-0

White expects Black to castle K-side and hopes that he will then be able to storm the castled position.

7 ... 0-0

8 f2-f4

White begins the assault, but perhaps he should have developed his K-side pieces first.

8 ... d7-d5

Black wants to open the centre and use his bishops to rake across the board at the white king.

The bishop takes up a fine attacking post, threatening c2, and working well with his colleague on g7.

11	Bc4-b3	Ne7xd5
12	Nc3xd5	Nb4xd5

Black has regained his pawn, his bishops have fine diagonals onto the white king's position, and the white queen is en prise.

13	Qe3-f3	Qd8-f6

Black's power on the diagonals is complete; he threatens 14 ... Qf6xb2 mate.

14   c2-c3

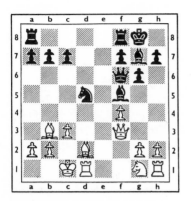

White blocks the dark-squared diagonal, but opens up the light-squared one! Now the white king is a prisoner, there is nowhere he can go. Black surveys the trapped king and seizes his chance.

14   ...   Nd5-b4

The knight can't be taken: 15 c3xb4 Qf6xb2 mate. Now that the white king is trapped Black stops at nothing to get at him.

15   Bb3-c4   Qf6-a6!!

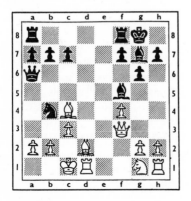

A master stroke! Black takes full advantage of the unhappy position of the white king. If now 16 Bc4xa6 Nb4xa2 is mate!

16   g2-g4

White tries to rid himself of the wretched black bishop and hopes that he will get some elbow room for his king.

16   ...   Qa6xa2

Again Black finds a brilliant way of taking advantage of the net his pieces have woven around the white king.

17   Bd2-e3

There is nothing else: (a) 17 g4xf5 Qa2-a1 mate, (b) 17 c3xb4 Qa2-b1 mate, (c) 17 Bc4xa2 Nb4xa2 mate, and (d) 17 Bd2-e1 Qa2-b1+ 18 Kc1-d2 Qb1-c2+ 19 Kd2-e3 Rf8-e8+, and mate soon follows.

17   ...   Bg7xc3!

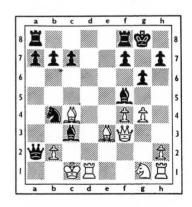

Leaving his queen en prise for the third time, Black finally carries out the execution.

18   b2xc3   Qa2-c2 mate

The lesson to be learnt from both these games is obvious: if a king is trapped in a corner, look out for a checkmate.

Snap mates can occur anywhere on the board when a king runs short of escape squares. We have looked at three positions and two games, and the position of the trapped king was different in each case. However, there are two special cases which you should know: *smothered mate* and *the back rank*

SMOTHERED MATE

When a king is completely surrounded by his own pieces he has nowhere to move; he cannot breathe; he is smothered. If an enemy knight attacks him and cannot be captured then it is check mate—smothered mate. There are two places in which this is likely to happen: in the centre, and in a corner. Smothered mate in the centre normally arises in the opening; so we shall deal with that first:

Game 19
(Caro-Kann Defence)

1	e2-e4	c7-c6
2	d2-d4	d7-d5
3	Nb1-c3	d5xe4
4	Nc3xe4	Nb8-d7

Black wants to develop his king's knight to f6. If he does so right away, then White can play 5 Ne4xf6+, and Black will have to recapture with a pawn, which will leave him with doubled pawns on the f-file.

But Black has allowed his king to be surrounded by his own pieces.

5 Qd1-e2
This seems silly; White deliberately shuts in his king's bishop. But White is setting a trap . . .

5 . . .   Ng8-f6?
. . . into which Black falls!

6 Ne4-d6 mate

Trapped by his own pieces, the black king has nowhere to run.

The ingredients needed for this mate are a queen or a rook on the half-open e-file, and a knight able to hop into the attack. Normally the knight mates as above, on the d-file, but sometimes the f-file can provide the mating square.

Game 20
(Queen's Gambit—Albin Counter Gambit)

1	d2-d4	d7-d5
2	c2-c4	e7-e5
3	d4xe5	d5-d4
4	Ng1-f3	Nb8-c6
5	g2-g3	Bf8-b4+
6	Bc1-d2	

6 ...   Qd8-e7

... the black queen takes up station on the e-file.

7 a2-a3   Nc6xe5

8 Bd2xb4?

White thinks he is safe because he is attacking the black queen.

8 ...   Ne5xf3 mate

Now the white king is completely shut in by his own pieces so ...

This is not a true smothered mate, because the king does have the square d2; so he is not completely smothered by his own pieces. However, the idea is exactly the same. When your king has not castled and is hemmed in by your own pieces, always be on the look out for a queen coming to the e-file, and then a knight delivering the deadly check.

Game 21
(Giuoco Piano)

1	e2-e4	e7-e5
2	Ng1-f3	Nb8-c6
3	Bf1-c4	Bf8-c5
4	0-0	Ng8-f6
5	Rf1-e1	0-0
6	c2-c3	

White intends to advance his d-pawn and win space in the centre.

6	...	Qd8-e7
7	d2-d4	e5xd4
8	e4-e5	Nf6-g4
9	c3xd4	

White seems to have achieved his target; his pawns stand proud in the middle, Black's pieces are being driven around, and the white pieces are ready to race out and take advantage of the extra space.
Black suddenly turns the tables:

9	...	Nc6xd4!

A splendid sacrifice to pull the white knight away from the K-side.

10	Nf3xd4	Qe7-h4

Black has the double threat, f2 and h2. One of the white pawns must fall.

11	Nd4-f3	

White prefers to hold on to his h-pawn, and he hopes the knight will help protect his K-side.

11	...	Qh4xf2+
12	Kg1-h1	

The king is chased into the corner.

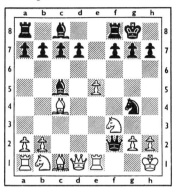

Black now finds the key move:

12	...	Qf2-g1+!

White must capture.

13	Re1xg1	

Taking with the knight is exactly the same.

13	...	Ng4-f2 mate

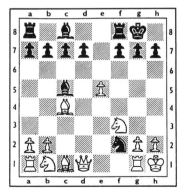

The king, surrounded by his own bodyguard, has been smothered, and the knight was on hand to deal the death blow.

If you allow your king to be smothered in the centre, then there is no excuse: you have simply dug your own grave. In such positions, your king has nowhere to move, and you should take very good care that he can't be mated. Smothered mate in the corner is different. In Game 19 for example, the mate was quite a thunderbolt; Black had to find the brilliant queen sacrifice. The white king seemed to be quite safe on move 11, and mate must have come as a horrible shock. You cannot prepare yourself to meet a shock; all you can do is remember to think hard about the safety of your king at every move. In that way you won't get so many shocks!

THE BACK RANK

This is every junior's nightmare! Every chess player at one time or another has fallen into the back rank trap. Look at this diagram.

Didn't you feel stupid when your opponent gleefully seized his rook, rammed it down the board, and you realized what you had done?

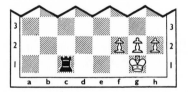

Don't you recognize the position? Haven't there been several occasions when your king has sat 'safely' behind that line of pawns? And wasn't there a game where you were busily bashing your opponent at the other end of the board, and forgot about your own king?

Yes, it has happened to everybody!

The back rank is always a target for attacks; the king standing behind its pawn shield seems safe, but all his 'safe' squares, f1, g1, and h1, are on the same line. Naturally then this line is a target for the enemy's heavy pieces.

A one-move snap mate on the back rank can only happen when one player makes a bad mistake. Yet there is far more to the back-rank threat than taking advantage of bad mistakes. Our first example shows a little combination, involving a queen sacrifice.

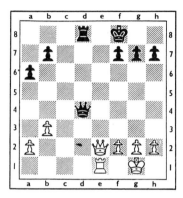

White to move

1 Qe2-e7+

The king is forced further behind the pawns.

1 ...   Kf8-g8

2 Qe7-e8+!

The point! White will lose his queen for a rook, but Black loses something more important: control over his back rank.

2 ...   Rd8xe8

3 Re1xe8 mate

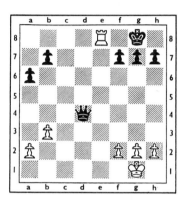

Open files and a weak back line are the keys to the back-rank mate.

Our second example is more than a little combination. This position occurred in a game between two grandmasters.

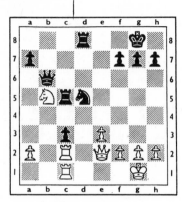

White to move

Black's passed pawn on c3 has been a thorn in White's side for some time now. At last White sees the chance to rid himself of this nuisance.

1 Nb5xc3

Why not? The pawn is attacked three times and defended only twice.

1 ...   **Nd5xc3**

2 Rc2xc3   **Rc5xc3**

3 Rc1xc3

Now the air has cleared, and White has won his pawn. Both kings are trapped on the back ranks, and there are plenty of open files. The black king is safe enough, with his rook

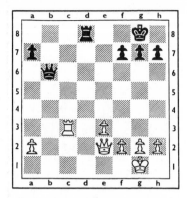

patrolling the back line, and before he won the pawn White carefully calculated that Black cannot now play 3 . . . Qb6-b1+ 4 Qe2-f1 Rd8-d1, because of 5 Rc3-c8 mate. White sat back, satisfied with himself. A moment later he wished he had stayed at home!

3 ...   **Qb6-b2!**

4 White resigns

Slowly it dawns on White that he has lost a rook. If (a) 4 Qe2xb2 Rd8-d1 mate, or (b) 4 Qe2-e1 Qb2xc3 5 Qe1xc3 Rd8-d1 mates, or (c) 4 Rc3-c2 Qb2-b1+, whilst his own try at being clever (d) 4 Rc3-c8 Qb2-b1+ 5 Qe2-f1 Qb1xf1+ 6 Kg1xf1 Rd8xc8, is equally useless.

Black made good use of his open files and took advantage of White's weakness on the back rank.

In our third example we see Richard Réti in action again, this time as White, against the Russian master Bogoljuboff. The middle game is a scramble in the centre; a muddle that Réti brings to an end by exchanging men, opening lines, and attacking the back rank.

Game 22
(Réti's Opening)

Réti	Bogoljuboff
1 Ng1-f3	Ng8-f6
2 c2-c4	e7-e6
3 g2-g3	d7-d5
4 Bf1-g2	Bf8-d6
5 0-0	0-0
6 b2-b3	Nb8-d7
7 Bc1-b2	

12 f2-f3

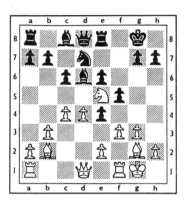

Réti's minor pieces all have good squares; now he wants to clear up the centre position before deciding what to do with his heavy brigade.

12 ...   e4xf3

13 Bg2xf3
This is better than recapturing with the pawn: the f-file is open from White's side, and Black's troubles are just beginning.

13 ...   Qd8-c7

14 Ne5xd7
A pity, but the knight couldn't be supported on its splendid central outpost.

14 ...   Bc8xd7

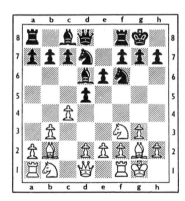

Réti waits before throwing forward his centre pawns. He wants to see where Bogoljuboff will develop the black pieces before committing himself.

7 ...	Rf8-e8
8 d2-d4	c7-c6
9 Nb1-d2	Nf6-e4
10 Nd2xe4	d5xe4
11 Nf3-e5	.f7-f5

15 e2-e4
Black is a little cramped, so Réti expands the centre pawns, hoping to gain more ground.

15 . . . e6-e5

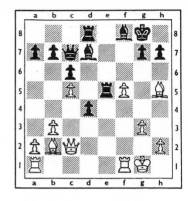

20 Bb2xd4 Re5xf5
21 Rf1xf5 Bd7xf5
22 Qc2xf5 Rd8xd4
23 Ra1-f1

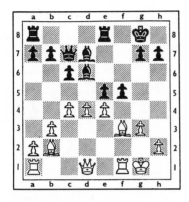

Bogoljuboff doesn't like the idea of being squashed, so he fights back in the centre.

16 c4-c5 Bd6-f8
17 Qd1-c2 e5xd4
18 e4xf5 Ra8-d8
19 Bf3-h5!
A splendid move; Réti attacks the rook, and fixes his eye on f7.

19 . . . Re8-e5
The vital point of the game has been reached. (*See Diagram*)

The black king is in trouble on the open diagonal from c4. Réti can see that he might get a piece onto f7, and if he can get that far, then perhaps f8 and the back rank will be threatened. First, Réti must open the files for attack.

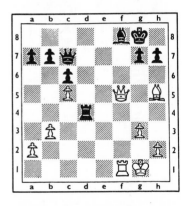

Réti takes complete control of the open f-file, and the back rank comes under immediate fire.

23 . . . Rd4-d8
The rook has to retreat and give support to Black's weak back line. If (a) 23 . . . Qc7-d8 24 Qf5-f7+ Kg8-h8 25 Qf7xf8+ Qd8xf8 26 Rf1xf8 mate, or (b) 23 . . . Bf8-e7

24 Qf5-f7+ Kg8-h8   25 Qf7-f8+ Be7xf8   26 Rf1xf8 mate, or (c) 23 . . . Qc7-e7   24 Bh5-f7+ Kg8-h8 25 Bf7-d5 (threatening 26 Qf5xf8+) Qe7-f6   26 Qf5-c8, and in each case it is the back line that brings about Black's downfall.

24   Bh5-f7+

Forcing the black king into the corner, and away from the defence of f8.

24   . . .   Kg8-h8

25   Bf7-e8!

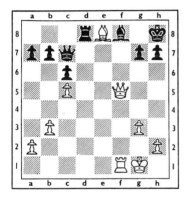

Again mate is threatened on f8: 25 . . . Rd8xe8   26 Qf5xf8+ etc.

Black has to give up a piece, but he is still mated.

25   . . .   h7-h6

26   Qf5xf8+   Kh8-h7

27   Be8-g6+!

Réti finds a neat finish.

27   . . .   Kh7xg6

28   Qf8-f5 mate

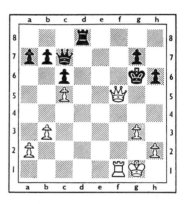

Mate did not occur on the back rank, yet it was the weakness on Black's back line that Réti seized upon, and it was his pressure there, his threats of mate, which won the game for him.

SUMMARY

Whenever a king is boxed in you should think of him as a prisoner in his cell, awaiting execution.

If it is your king then an alarm bell should go off in your mind. Remember that one check may be enough to finish you off. Remember that no matter how easily you may appear to be winning, no matter how many pieces ahead you may be, one slip can cost you your king. Always think those extra few seconds before you move; make sure your king is safe. It may seem a waste of time, it may even *be* a waste of time, but make sure. Then you won't get the shock that the elderly gentleman gave to Bobby Blunder.

If it is your opponent's king who is imprisoned, then the axe is in your hands. Can you get at the enemy king to deliver the final blow? Can you get at him on the back row? Can you tighten the screw further so that there are no squares left for him to escape? David beat Goliath with a one-off shot. He was lucky; if he had missed, the giant would surely have cut him apart. You must always be on the look out for that one-off shot, that thunderbolt from nowhere that mates the enemy king. Yet you must not rely upon being lucky. You must work hard to get at a prisoner king and make his final moves of life as uncomfortable as possible.

5 Checkmate!

Checkmate can occur anywhere at any time; no matter where the king may be he is always in danger of a surprise attack. However, there are several checkmates which crop up frequently, and it is well worth your while to know them.

In each case we shall look at a typical position; you won't be likely to reach exactly the same position, but you may well get something similar. To make it easier to follow we shall allow White to win every time; and sometimes we shall only draw part of the diagram or show just the important pieces.

CHECKMATE IN THE OPENING

CHECKMATE!   *CHECKMATE!*

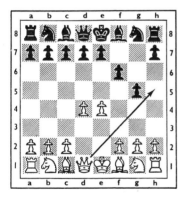   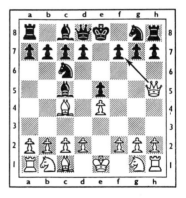

White to move plays **Qd1-h5 mate**   White to move plays **Qh5xf7 mate**

Fool's Mate   *Scholar's Mate*

Checkmate

THE KING IN THE CENTRE

White to move plays
1 Qd1-e2   Bc8-g4
2 Nе4xf6 mate

CHECKMATE!

CHECKMATE!

White to move plays
1 Bc1-g5   Qf6-g6
2 Rd1-d8 mate

THE CASTLED KING

When the king has castled K-side and stands behind a line of pawns the squares g7 and h7 are the natural targets. h7 is the easier square to attack, but it is also easier for Black to defend (he may well have a knight on f6).

CHECKMATE!   *CHECKMATE!*

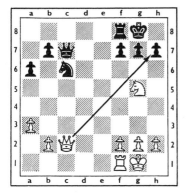   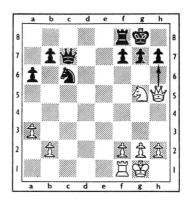

White to move plays **Qc2xh7 mate**   White to move plays **Qh5xh7 mate**

CHECKMATE!   *CHECKMATE!*

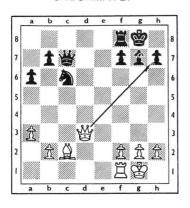   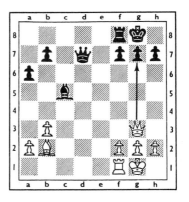

White to move plays **Qd3xh7 mate**   White to move plays **Qg3xg7 mate**

Checkmate

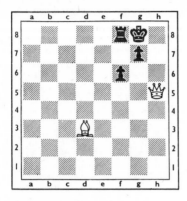

White to move plays

1 Bd3-h7+   Kg8-h8
2 Bh7-g6+   Kh8-g8
3 Qh5-h7 mate

CHECKMATE!

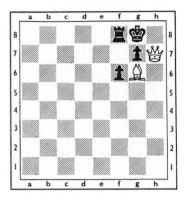

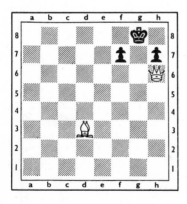

White to move plays

1 Bd3xh7+   Kg8-h8
2 Bh7-g6+   Kh8-g8
3 Qh6-h7+   Kg8-f8
4 Qh7xf7 mate

CHECKMATE!

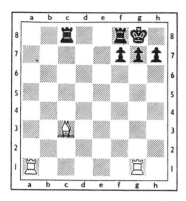

White to move plays

1 Rg1xg7+   Kg8-h8
2 Rg7-g8++   Kh8xg8
3 Ra1-g1 mate

CHECKMATE!

Pillsbury's Mate

White to move plays

1 Rg1xg7+   Kg8-h8
2 Rg7xf7+   Kh8-g8
3 Rf7-g7+   Kg8-h8
4 Rg7-g1+   Rf8-f6
5 Bc3xf6 mate

CHECKMATE!

THE h-FILE

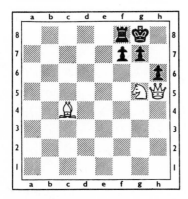

White to move plays

1 Bc4xf7+ Kg8-h8
2 Qh5-g6 h6xg5
3 Qg6-h5 mate

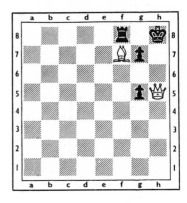

CHECKMATE!

Greco's Mate

White to move plays

1 Nd5-e7+ Kg8-h8
2 Rh1xh7+ Kh8xh7
3 Ra1-h1 mate

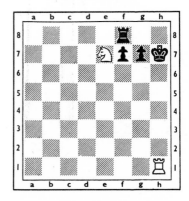

CHECKMATE!

Anastasia's Mate

THE FIANCHETTO POSITION

Often the pawn shield in front of the king is weakened by the g-pawn having advanced to g6; perhaps Black fianchettoed his bishop, or maybe he wanted to block the diagonal leading to h7. In this case the long dark-squared diagonal becomes important, and g7 and h8 are targets.

CHECKMATE!   *CHECKMATE!*

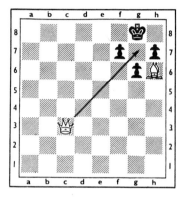   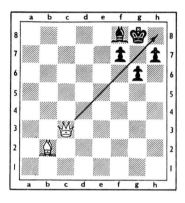

White to move plays **Qc3-g7 mate**   White to move plays **Qc3-h8 mate**

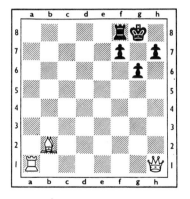

White to move plays

1	Qh1xh7+	Kg8xh7
2	Ra1-h1+	Kh7-g8
3	Rh1-h8 mate	

CHECKMATE!

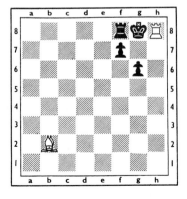

Mayet's Mate

Checkmate

When attacking the fianchetto position it is often useful to have a pawn on f6; Black must then prevent the white queen from getting to g7.

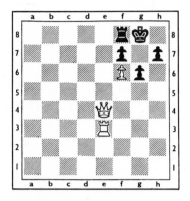

White to move plays

1 Qe4-f4   Kg8-h8
2 Qh4-h6   Rf8-g8
3 Re3-h3 and mate next move

CHECKMATE!

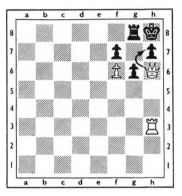

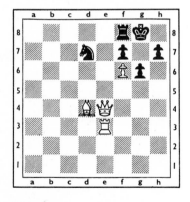

White to move plays

1 Qe4-f4   Kg8-h8
2 Qf4-h6   Rf8-g8
Now if 3 Re3-h3, Black defends h7
by 3 . . . Nd7-f8; so
3 Qh6xh7+   Kh8xh7
4 Re3-h3 mate

CHECKMATE!

Lolli's Mate

THE MINOR PIECES

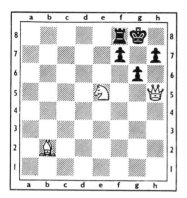

White to move plays
1 Ne5-g4   g6xh5
2 Ng4-h6 mate

CHECKMATE!

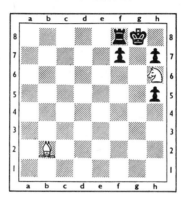

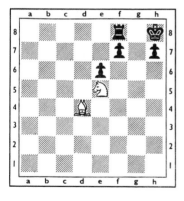

White to move plays
1 Ne5-g6++   Kh8-g8
2 Ng6-e7 mate

CHECKMATE!

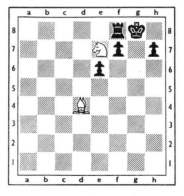

THE BACK RANK

White to move plays
1 Bc1-h6   Rf8-d8
2 Re2-e8+   Rd8xe8
3 Re1xe8 mate

CHECKMATE!

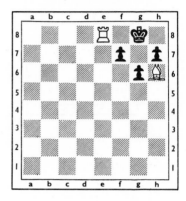

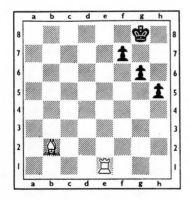

White to move plays
1 Re1-e8+   Kg8-h7
2 Re8-h8 mate

CHECKMATE!

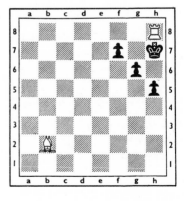

OTHER MATES OF THE CASTLED KING

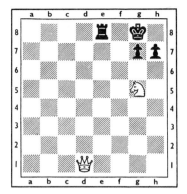

White to move plays

1	Qd1-d5+	Kg8-h8
2	Ng5-f7 +	Kh8-g8
3	Nf7-h6++	Kg8-h8
4	Qd5-g8+	Re8xg8
5	Nh6-f7 mate	

CHECKMATE!

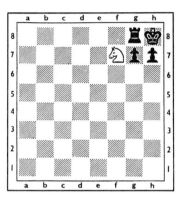

Philidor's Lecacy

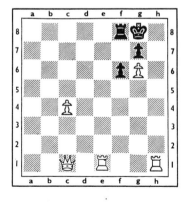

White to move plays

1	Rh1-h8+	Kg8xh8
2	Re1-h1+	Kh8-g8
3	Rh1-h8+	Kg8xh8
4	Qc1-h1+	Kh8-g8
5	Qh1-h7 mate	

CHECKMATE!

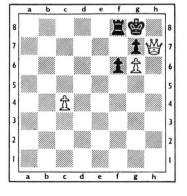

Damiano's Mate

THE Q-SIDE CASTLED KING

A possibility here is Boden's Mate; this can come about in two ways:

White to move plays
1 Qc3xc6+   b7xc6
2 Be2-a6 mate

CHECKMATE!

Boden's Mate   A

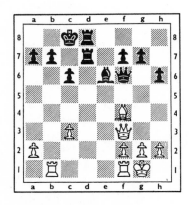

White to move plays
1 Qf3xc6+   b7xc6
2 Rb1-b8 mate

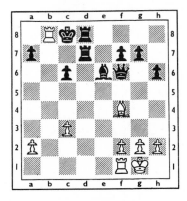

CHECKMATE!

Boden's Mate   B

OTHER MATING POSITIONS

CHECKMATE!

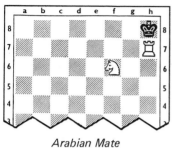

Arabian Mate

CHECKMATE!

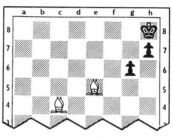

Bishop Mate

CHECKMATE!

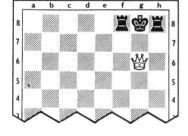

CHECKMATE!

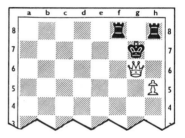

CHECKMATE!

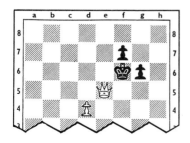

CHECKMATE!

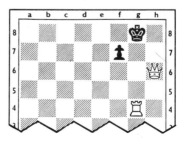

BUILDING A KING ATTACK

6 Attacking the king in the opening

IN THE OPENING YOU SHOULD BE DEVELOPING YOUR PIECES, NOT ATTACKING THE KING

We all dream of an immediate slashing attack right from the first move. Our pieces thunder across the board, seize the poor enemy king by the scruff of the neck, and wring the life out of him before he realizes what is happening. Checkmate; the opponent dead and buried inside ten moves!

Marvellous, but like all dreams, it is only a dream; it doesn't happen very often.. Usually the quick attack comes to a sticky end. Your opponent sits back and beats off your threats while quietly developing his pieces. Then, as your attack fizzles out and you find yourself miles behind in development, your opponent is ready to seize the advantage with a counter-attack.

The simplest form of the quick attack is the four-move or Scholar's Mate, 1 e2-e4 e7-e5 2 Bf1-c4 Bf8-c5 3 Qd1-h5, when Black is supposed to notice that his e-pawn is en prise and defend it by a move such as 3 . . . Nb8-c6, whereupon White plays 4 Qh5xf7 with great glee and announces checkmate. You may wonder why this is called Scholar's Mate. Black is quite obviously a fool! Not only does he get himself mated, but he misses a splendid opportunity of punishing White for attacking far too early. See now what happens when Black defends himself properly.

Game 23

1	e2-e4	e7-e5
2	Bf1-c4	Nb8-c6
3	Qd1-f3	

White threatens mate on f7, but his queen has been brought out far too soon.

| 3 | . . . | Ng8-f6 |

Black meets the threat with simple development.

| 4 | g2-g4 | |

White sets out to attack the knight which stands in his way.

| 4 | . . . | Bf8-c5 |
| 5 | g4-g5 | Nc6-d4! |

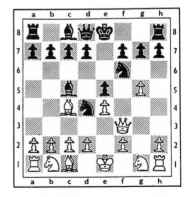

The other black knight takes a fine central square and drives White's queen from her menacing position.

6 Qf3-d3

Forced; White has to defend both his c-pawn and his e-pawn.

6 ...   Nf6-g4

7 f2-f3   d7-d5

8 e4xd5   Bc8-f5

A fine move, developing and gaining time by threatening the white queen. Now it is Black who is attacking, and his attack is more powerful because he has developed his pieces properly.

9 Qd3-c3   Bc5-b4!

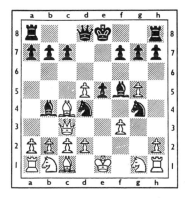

The wretched queen cannot find peace anywhere! If she captures the bishop by 10 Qc3xb4, then 10 . . . Nd4xc2+ forks king, queen, and rook.

10 Bc4-b5+   c7-c6

11 Qc3-c4

The only square.

11 ...   c6xb5

12 Qc4-f1

Once again the only square—how the white queen must wish that she had stayed at home!

12 ...   Nd4xc2+

13 Ke1-d1

Or 13 Ke1-e2 Qd8xd5, threatening to check on d3 and win the white queen.

13 ...   Qd8xd5

14 White resigns

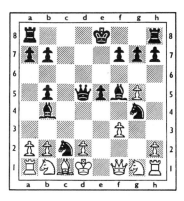

The black pieces have finally caught up with the white queen—this time there is no escape. The immediate threat is for one of the knights to check upon e3 when White loses his queen, because his d-pawn is pinned. None of White's possible moves saves him from disaster:

(a) 14 Qf1-g2 Ng4-e3+,

(b) 14 Qf1-h3 Ng4-f2+,

(c) 14 Kd1-e2 Bf5-d3+,

(d) 14 d2-d4 Ng4-e3+ 15 Bc1xe3, Nc2xe3, and

(e) 14 Qf1-e2 Ng4-e3+.

To attempt a snap mate in the opening is very silly. You cannot hope to be successful unless your opponent blunders. If your opponent is a stronger player, then like Black in Game 23 he will just casually brush your attack aside, develop rapidly, and walk all over you! You should always be on the look-out for the possibility of a quick mate at both ends of the board, but you must remember that your first aim in a game of chess is to bring out your pieces onto squares where they can join together to attack the enemy with their full force.

THE KING HUNT

The only real chance you will get of launching a mating attack in the opening, is if your opponent's king comes out into the open. Then you may be able to start a king hunt. Look at Game 24.

Game 24
(King's Gambit)

1	e2-e4	e7-e5
2	f2-f4	e5xf4
3	Ng1-f3	Bf8-e7
4	Bf1-c4	Ng8-f6
5	Nb1-c3	Nf6xe4

6	Bc4xf7+	Ke8xf7
7	Nc3xe4	d7-d5

Black stakes a claim for his share of the centre.

8	Nf3-e5+	Kf7-e6

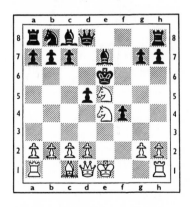

Black takes the opportunity to re-move White's strong central pawn. He hopes for 6 Nc3xe4 d7-d5, when he will regain his piece, and have open lines and space for his men, but White doesn't intend to let Black have his way.

The king could have retreated safely to g8, but Black decides to make a bold effort to win one of the white knights.

9 Qd1-g4+

The black king is in the open and the hunt begins.

| 9 | ... | Ke6xe5 |

| 10 | d2-d4+ | Ke5xd4 |

Not 10 . . . Ke5xe4 11 Qg4xf4 mate. The black king is finding it easy to march up the board, but will he find it as easy to go home again?

| 11 | c2-c3+ | Kd4-e5 |

Black is mated if he tries anything else: (a) 11 . . . Kd4-d3 12 Qg4-e2 mate, (b) 11 . . . Kd4-c4 12 Qg4-e2 mate, (c) 11 . . . Kd4xe4 12 Qg4xf4+ Ke4-d3 13 Qf4-d4+ Kd3-c2 14 Qd4-d2 mate.

| 12 | Qg4xf4+ | Ke5-e6 |

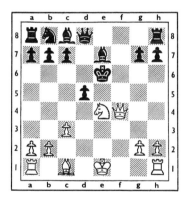

White is the huntsman; his pieces are the hounds. The black king is the fox desperately trying to get back to his hole.

| 13 | 0-0! | |

After five consecutive checks White leaves the black king in peace for a moment. Yet, he still threatens 14 Qf4-f5 mate!

| 13 | ... | d5xe4 |

| 14 | Qf4-f5+ | Ke6-d6 |

| 15 | Rf1-d1+ | Kd6-c6 |

| 16 | Qf5xe4+ | |

White doesn't bother to take the black queen; he's after bigger game.

| 16 | ... | Kc6-b6 |

| 17 | Bc1-e3+ | |

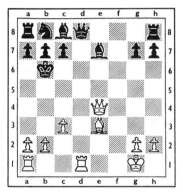

Another white hound joins the attack; the fox is not going to be allowed a moment's rest.

| 17 | ... | Be7-c5 |

| 18 | Qe4-b4+ | |

White takes advantage of the pin on Black's bishop to bring his queen closer to her quarry.

| 18 | ... | Kb6-a6 |

Not 18 . . . Kb6-c6 19 Qb4xc5 mate.

| 19 | Qb4-a4+ | Ka6-b6 |

| 20 | Be3xc5+ | Kb6xc5 |

The black king has no choice other than to go where the white pieces chase him.

| 21 | b2-b4+ | |

Now the white pawns start to snap and snarl at Black's heels.

| 21 | ... | Kc5-c4 |

If 21 . . . Kc5-b6 22 Qa4-a5+ Kb6-c6 23 Qa5-c5 mate.

22	Qa4-b3+	Kc4-b5
23	a2-a4+	Kb5-b6

25	Qb3-a4+	Kb5-c4
26	b4-b5+	Kc4xc3
27	Ra1-c1+	Kc3-b2
28	Rc1-c2 mate	

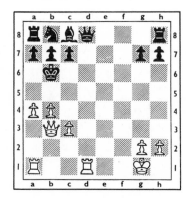

There is no saving the black king:
23 ... Kb5-a6 24 b4-b5+ Ka6-b6
25 a4-a5+ Kb6-c5 26 Qb3-b4
mate.

24 a4-a5+   Kb6-b5

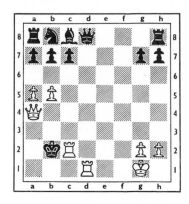

After 21 checks the black king has
been run to ground!

The idea of the king hunt is simple. A king is usually well-defended behind his pawn shield; so drag him out into the open! Then your opponent's pieces won't be in a position to help him, and your men will be free to direct their full power in attack. The chase is on, with the king skating round the board in search of a home, and your pieces in hot pursuit trying to nail him before he finds safety.

Game 24 was exciting, but it was also unusual. You must not expect to be able to develop just one or two pieces, sacrifice one of them to bring the enemy king into the open, and then drive the king around the board until you mate him.

A king hunt is a power mate. Even after the king has been brought into mid-board he will be mated only if the attacking pieces are far stronger than those that can defend him. If you start a king hunt in the opening, your undeveloped pieces must be able to race quickly into attacking position; if they can be developed with check, then so much the better. Similarly you must not allow your opponent time to defend himself by bringing his undeveloped pieces into play.

The next two games—25 and 26—show just how important the development of the pieces really is for the success or failure of a king hunt. The same opening was played in both games, and we can see how accurate you have to be if you want to hunt down the enemy king.

Game 25

(*Two Knights Defence*)

1	e2-e4	e7-e5
2	Ng1-f3	Nb8-c6
3	Bf1-c4	Ng8-f6
4	Nf3-g5	d7-d5
5	e4xd5	Nf6xd5

A safer method of defence is 5 . . . Nc6-a5 6 Bc4-b5+ c7-c6 7 d5xc6 b7xc6, when Black has free play and open lines in return for his pawn.

6   Ng5xf7

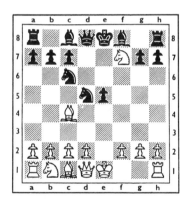

White seizes his chance to expose the black king.

6   . . .   Ke8xf7

7   Qd1-f3+

Now Black is in check, and his knight on d5 is pinned, and threatened a second time.

7   . . .   Kf7-e6

Black has little choice. If he gives back the knight, 7 . . . Kf7-e8 8 Bc4xd5, then he is a pawn down and has lost the right to castle.

8   Nb1-c3

The knight on d5 is still pinned; so White attacks it again.

8   . . .   Nc6-b4

This is the important position.

The black king is in the open. Can White catch him? Remember, he must try to bring his pieces into the attack quickly; Black must complete his development and try to find a safe home for his king. Remember also, Black has an extra piece. If White does not get something in return, then he will lose.

9   0-0

This looks like a good start. White has defended himself against the threat of 9 . . . Nb4xc2+, and is ready to bring his rook into action along the e-file.

9   . . .   c7-c6

Black props up his central knight, and leaves his king free to find safety.

10   d2-d4   Ke6-d6

A piece for a pawn ahead, Black can afford to give back another pawn.

11   d4xe5+   Kd6-c7

12   Rf1-d1   Bc8-e6

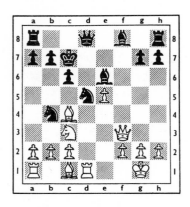

It is already clear that Black is winning the battle. White has managed to add only the rook to the force of his attack. Black meanwhile has supported his centre with pawn and bishop, and has found a fairly comfortable position for his king. Furthermore, he is still a knight ahead.

13   a2-a3   Qd8-h4

Indeed, it is Black who is now able to switch over to the attack!

14   Bc4-e2   Nd5xc3

15   Qf3xc3   Nb4-d5

In just seven moves White's attack has fallen apart, and it is Black who closes in for the kill.

16   Qc3-b3   Bf8-c5

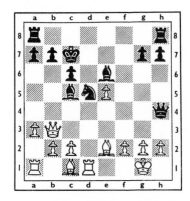

Splendid development with a threat against f2. The black pieces begin to pound away at White's K-side, and there is little to hold them back.

17   g2-g3   Qh4-h3

18   c2-c4

A piece down and under fire, White makes a despairing effort to get counter-play, but Black is not to be put off.

18   . . .   Rh8-f8

19   Rd1-f1   Nd5-f4!

Threatening 20 . . . Qh3-g2 mate.

20   Bc1xf4   Rf8xf4

The weight of the attacking forces is beginning to tell. The white g-pawn is pinned from queen to queen; so the rook cannot be taken.

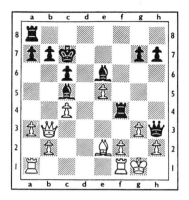

21	. . .	Be6xc4
22	g3xf4	Bc4-d5
23	Be2-f3	Bd5xf3
24	White resigns	

21 Qb3-d1
By unpinning his g-pawn White
prevents 21 . . . Rf4-h4 and 22 . . .
Qh3xh2 mate.

White must give up his queen to
stop mate on g2.

White's king hunt never really got started. At no time did it seem that he
was likely to get his pieces into play quickly enough to trouble the black
king. In fact the black pieces found time not only to cover their king, but
also to build up a counter-attack. Let us go back to the beginning and have
another try.

Game 26

(Two Knights Defence)

1	e2-e4	e7-e5
2	Ng1-f3	Nb8-c6
3	Bf1-c4	Ng8-f6
4	Nf3-g5	d7-d5
5	e4xd5	Nf6xd5
6	Ng5xf7	Ke8xf7
7	Qd1-f3+	Kf7-e6
8	Nb1-c3	Nc6-b4

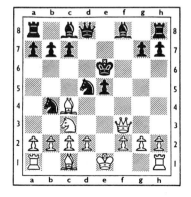

We have reached the same position as in Game 25. Last time White played 9 0-0, but couldn't get his pieces into the attack quickly enough. Can he find a better plan this time?

9 a2-a3

Black can now win the exchange, but White doesn't mind giving up more material provided he can get his remaining pieces into action.

9 . . .   Nb4xc2+

10 Ke1-d1

The white king makes room for the rook to come to e1.

10 . . .   Nc2xa1

Perhaps Black would do better to play 10 . . . Nc2-d4 so that his knight can help his king, but White regains his piece with 11 Bc4x d5+, and still has the attack.

11 Nc3xd5   Ke6-d6

Black must not allow a discovered check.

12 d2-d4   c7-c6

13 Bc1-f4!

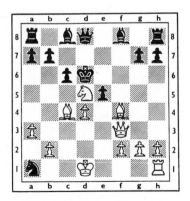

White is clearly doing much better than in Game 25. He has four pieces in action, and the rook waiting in the wings has a ready-made square on e1. Black in contrast has not managed to develop his pieces, and his knight has wandered away from the scene of battle.

13 . . .   e5xf4

Taking the knight would have been disastrous: 13 . . . c6xd5 14 Qf3xd5+ Kd6-e7 15 Bf4-g5+ Ke7-e8 16 Qd5-f7 mate.

14 Qf3xf4+   Kd6-d7

15 Rh1-e1

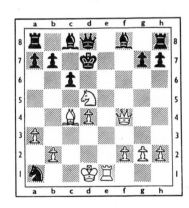

The king hunt is in full swing; all of White's pieces have reached battle stations.

15 . . .   Qd8-a5

Black gives his king some room. This is his only chance, for if
(a) 15 . . . c6xd5 16 Bc4-b5 mate,
(b) 15 . . . Bf8-d6 16 Qf4-f5 mate,
or (c) 15 . . . Bf8-e7 16 Re1xe7+ Qd8xe7 17 Qf4-c7+ and 18 Qc7xe7.

16	Qf4-f5+	Kd7-d8
17	Qf5-g5+	Kd8-d7
18	Re1-e7+!	

a rook and bishop behind, and must catch the king.

20 Rf7xf8+   Ke8xf8

Black is mated whatever he does:
(a) 20 . . . Rh8xf8 21 Qg5-e7 mate,
or (b) 20 . . . Ke8-d7 21 Qg5-e7
mate.

21   Qg5-e7+   Kf8-g8

22   Nd5-f6 mate

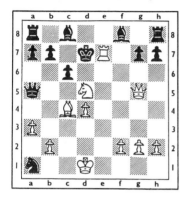

18   . . .   Kd7-d8

Or 18 . . . Kd7-d6 19 Qg5-e5 mate;
or 18 . . . Bf8xe7 19 Qg5xe7 mate.

19   Re7-f7+   Kd8-e8

Black clings on desperately. White is

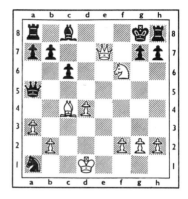

In Game 26 White found a way of bringing his pieces rapidly into action, and by pounding relentlessly at the black king he gave his opponent no chance to complete his own development.

There is little possibility of a power mate in the opening. The king is usually too well defended in his own camp, and you can't get your pieces out quickly enough to overpower him. However, you may sometimes be able to drag your opponent's king into open country at the beginning of the game. This gives you a chance; but if you are going to hunt him down, then you must do so with the greatest possible energy. Games 25 and 26 show how the result is balanced on a knife edge. Once you have got your teeth into the king you must cling on tight and never let go. Your pieces must tear him to bits; he must never be allowed a moment's peace, or else he may find time to defend himself.

f7, A TARGET FOR ATTACK

Have you noticed the importance of the square f7 in all four games in this chapter? In Game 23 White played 2 Bf1-c4 and 3 Qd1-f3 and hoped he would be able to mate with the queen on f7. In Games 24, 25, and 26, White sacrificed on f7 to draw the black king out into the open. Why is the square f7 so important?

Look at the row of black pawns standing ready for the game to begin. How is each pawn defended?

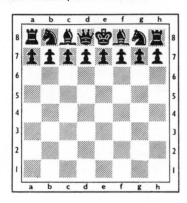

a7 and h7 are each defended by a rook.

b7 and g7 are each guarded by a bishop.

c7 is held safely by the queen.

d7 and e7 are each strongly protected.

But f7 is defended only by the king.

The square f7 is the weak point in Black's defence. How can White attack it? The following diagrams show the lines of attack.

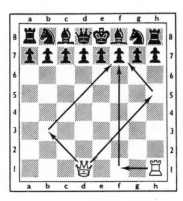

The queen is the most powerful piece for an opening attack on f7. She has three squares, b3, f3, and h5, which she can get to fairly easily.

The rook is the most difficult piece to bring into the attack, because he has only one line of approach, and the f-pawn must first be cleared out of the way.

Attack of queen and rook

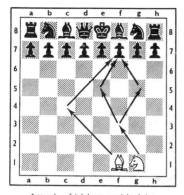

Attack of bishop and knight

The bishop attacks f7 from its natural development square, c4.

The king's knight is normally developed at f3, and can then join the attack by moving to e5 or g5.

In games beginning 1 e2-e4 e7-e5, the most important of the attacking lines is the diagonal from c4 to f7, because the white bishop develops easily to c4, and Black cannot block the diagonal by putting a pawn on e6.

Once Black has played . . . e7-e5, his best defensive piece for f7 is his king's knight. Although the knight can go to h6 (from where it will directly defend f7) this is a poor square for the piece. The knight does not want to be stuck at the edge of the board, from where he can't attack the centre, and White may easily remove him completely by playing Bc1xh6, at the same time shattering Black's K-side pawns. The black knight is much more active on f6, and although he does not directly defend f7, he does block two of White's lines of approach.

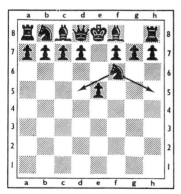

The king's knight defends from f6.

The black knight blocks a White attack along the f-file, and prevents the white queen from moving to h5. The knight also supports a possible . . . d7-d5 which will block the white bishop's diagonal.

The weakness of f7 is obvious in e-pawn openings, but no matter how a game begins you must always remember that until you have castled the square will be a weak spot in your defence. Game 27 is remarkable! It was never played. The Russian Grandmaster David Bronstein went to bed one night and had a dream. Game 27 is Bronstein's dream game!

Game 27

(Nimzo-Indian Defence)

1	d2-d4	Ng8-f6
2	c2-c4	e7-e6
3	Nb1-c3	Bf8-b4
4	Bc1-g5	h7-h6
5	Bg5-h4	Qd8-e7
6	Ng1-f3	d7-d6
7	Qd1-a4+	

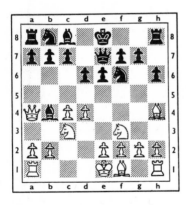

The black bishop is loose; so White begins action on the Q-side.

7 ...   Nb8-c6

8 d4-d5

Black's Q-side pieces are tangled; the bishop is defended only by the knight, and the knight in turn is both pinned and attacked. Black looks sure to lose a piece.

8 ...   e6xd5

9 c4xd5   Qe7-e4!

A cunning way out! Black threatens 10 ... Bb4xc3+ 11 b2xc3 Qe4xa4, and also 10 ... Nf6xd5.

10 Nf3-d2

The only way to meet both threats, but now the black queen can set her sights on f2.

10 ...   Qe4xh4

11 d5xc6   0-0

12 a2-a3

The black bishop is in trouble yet again. 12 ... Bb4xc3 13 Qa4xh4 loses Black his queen, but he finds another resource based on attacking f2.

12 ...   Nf6-g4

13 g2-g3
White holds up Black's attack for
one move.

13 ...   Qh4-f6
Threatening f2 again.

14 a3xb4
The normal plan of blocking the
f-file with the knight is no good in
this position: 14 Nd2-f3 Bb4xc3+
15 b2xc3 Qf6xc3+, and then Black
takes the white rook with check
before saving his own knight.

14 ...   Qf6xf2+

15 Ke1-d1   b7-b5!

Black is planning to mate on d1;
before he carry out his plan he must
drag White's queen away from the
diagonal protecting d1.

16 Qa4-b3   Bc8-e6

17 Qb3-a3
Or 17 Nc3-d5 Be6xd5 18 Qb3xd5
Ng4-e3+ 19 Kd1-c1 Qf2-e1 mate.

17 ...   Ng4-e3+
Now the queen is out of the way
Black can get on with the job.

18 Kd1-c1   Qf2-e1+

19 Nc3-d1   Qe1xd1 mate

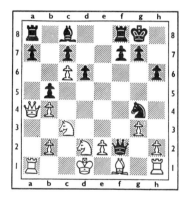
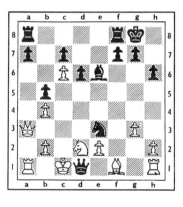

No doubt you find better things to dream about; but this is a remarkable
game all the same. David Bronstein is one of the most exciting players in
the history of chess. He revels in wild positions, and is a master of combin-
ations and sacrifices. The King's Gambit and other open games are his
favourite openings, because he likes to get to grips with his opponent right
from the word go. Years of experience in open positions have carved the
importance of f2 and f7 deeply on his mind. Even in a dream, even in a
d-pawn opening, everything clicked into place in his mind, just like a jig-
saw. White had a weakness at f2; how could he get at it? The grandmaster
has trained his mind to work like that. He knows automatically where to
look for weak spots, he understands the importance of f2 or f7 before a
king has castled; his mind is so well trained that he can do it in his sleep!

THE TEMPORARY BISHOP SACRIFICE ON f7

Earlier in this chapter we looked at several games in which White sacrificed a piece on f7, to draw the black king out into the open so that White could start a relentless king hunt. You must also look for the chance of a temporary bishop sacrifice on f7. You give up the bishop and then, by means of a fork or simple combination, regain your piece a few moves later. There are several ways in which this can happen.

Example 1

1	e2-e4	e7-e5
2	d2-d4	e5xd4
3	Bf1-c4	Bf8-c5
4	Bc4xf7+	Ke8xf7
5	Qd1-h5+	

Position after 5 Qd1-h5+

White will now regain his piece by playing 6 Qh5xc5, and then he has a good chance of winning the black pawn on d4. Frequently this little attack wins a pawn, but White is looking for more than just a material advantage. The black king remains stranded in the open and will never be able to castle into safety. White will have good chances of following up with a king attack, and Black may find that his king, lumbering around in the middle, gets in the way of his pieces. Example 2 shows just how the king may be caught.

Example 2—Game 28
(*English Opening*)

1	c2-c4	e7-e5
2	Ng1-f3	e5-e4
3	Nf3-d4	d7-d5
4	d2-d3	d5xc4
5	d3xc4	Bf8-c5
6	Nd4-b5	Bc5xf2+

(see diagram)

7	Ke1xf2	Qd8xd1
8	White resigns	

Position after 6 . . . Bc5xf2+

This time Black spotted that the white king was overloaded with work; he was defending f2 and d1. By sacrificing his bishop on f2, Black forced the king away from the more important job of defending his queen.

Example 3—Game 29
(*Modern Defence*)

1	e2-e4	g7-g6
2	d2-d4	Bf8-g7
3	Ng1-f3	d7-d6
4	Bf1-c4	Nb8-d7
5	Bc4xf7+	Ke8xf7
6	Nf3-g5+	Black resigns

Position after 6 Nf3-g5+

Yes, Black is lost already! If he retreats his king to either f8 or e8, then 7 Ng5-e6 wins his queen; and if he advances to f6, then 7 Qd1-f3 mate.

We have looked at three examples of a bishop sacrifice on f7 in the opening. Do not bother trying to learn them: the important thing is to remember to look for the possibility of a sacrifice whenever you have a bishop on c4. As a final example we shall look at yet another idea.

Example 4

1	e2-e4	c7-c5
2	Ng1-f3	d7-d6
3	Bf1-c4	Bc8-g4
4	Bc4xf7+	Ke8xf7
5	Nf3-g5+	
(see diagram)		
5	...	Kf7-e8
6	Qd1xg4	

Position after 5 Nf3-g5+

The black bishop on g4 was loose; by sacrificing, White was able to move his knight with check, and regain his piece. The result is very good for White: he has won a pawn, and Black having moved his king won't be able to castle.

Example 4 was a simple combination, one that is often possible when a black bishop on g4 is undefended. However there is another trap which is sometimes possible when the black bishop goes to g4; this involves a queen sacrifice, and is known as Légal's Mate.

f7, LEGAL'S MATE

Game 30 is a good example of this snap mate.

Game 30

(Scotch Gambit)

1	e2-e4	e7-e5
2	Ng1-f3	Nb8-c6
3	d2-d4	e5xd4
4	Bf1-c4	

White is in no hurry to regain his pawn; quick development is more important at this stage.

4	...	d7-d6

Very passive: Black shuts in his king's bishop.

5	c2-c3	

Because Black has taken up a cramped position White can well afford to sacrifice a pawn to gain extra space and a lead in development.

5	...	d4xc3
6	Nb1xc3	Bc8-g4
7	0-0	Nc6-e5

A poor move. Black wants to capture on f3 and double White's

pawns, but he is already two moves behind in development and by moving his knight again he wastes even more time. Furthermore White has a surprise up his sleeve.

8	Nf3xe5	Bg4xd1

Black would do better with 8 ... d6xe5 9 Qd1xg4, but then he would be a piece down without any compensation.

9	Bc4xf7+	

The road to f7 is open and White seizes his chance.

9	...	Ke8-e7
10	Nc3-d5 mate	

There are five squares open to the black king, but each one is covered by a white piece. This shows the basic pattern of Légal's Mate: the white queen is sacrificed, the f-pawn is captured, and the black king is encircled by White's minor pieces.

THE CASE OF THE MISSING f-PAWN

When the f-pawn has been moved, and the diagonal from h5 onto the king at e8 is open, a combination with the queen and knight is sometimes possible. You can see how this works in the diagram:

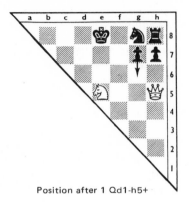

Position after 1 Qd1-h5+

Black's f-pawn has moved; so the white queen gives check when she arrives at h5. The obvious reply for Black is ... g7-g6, but this does not solve his problems.

1 ...   g7-g6

2 Ne5xg6!

Now the knight attacks the rook, and if 2 ... h7xg6 3 Qh5xh8; the rook goes anyway.

You must always keep this possibility in mind in any opening where the f-pawn has been moved.

Game 31

(Ruy López)

1	**e2-e4**	**e7-e5**
2	**Ng1-f3**	**Nb8-c6**
3	**Bf1-b5**	**f7-f5**

This is known as the Schliemann Defence; it is tricky: Black hopes to catch his opponent by surprise, but he is taking a risk by opening the diagonal from h5 to his king.

4	**d2-d4**	**f5xe4**
5	**Bb5xc6**	**b7xc6**
6	**Nf3xe5**	**d7-d5**
7	**Qd1-h5+**	**g7-g6**

There is nothing else: 7 ... Ke8-e7

8 Qh5-f7+ Ke7-d6 9 c2-c4 and the black king is trapped.

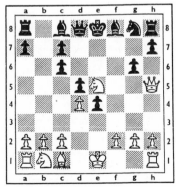

8	Ne5xg6	Ng8-f6

If 8 . . . h7xg6 9 Qh5xh8, White
has a rook and a pawn for his knight,
and much the better position.

9	Qh5-e5+	Bf8-e7
10	Ng6xh8	Ke8-f8

Black wants to win the cornered
knight, but his king is only march-
ing into the firing line.

11	Bc1-h6+	Kf8-g8
12	Qe5-g5+	Kg8xh8
13	Qg5-g7 mate	

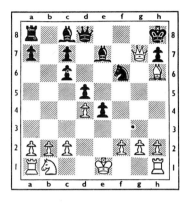

Black's king has killed himself! However, White was already a rook ahead,
and winning comfortably.

THE e-FILE, A LINE OF ATTACK

When the e-file is opened early in the game there is often a chance of winning material by catching the enemy king in the centre. Because he has the
first move and is therefore able to develop more aggressively, it is usually
White who gets the attacking chances, and Black who has to defend very
carefully. Whether you are White or Black, there are two rules which you
must follow when the e-file is open.

(a) Get your king out of the centre immediately.

(b) Put a rook on the file as soon as you can.

If you are careful you should never run into any trouble along the open
e-file; the problems that can arise are only little traps. There are two possible sources of danger: *discovered check*, and *the pin*.

DISCOVERED CHECK

Example 1—Game 32

(Petrov's Defence)

1	e2-e4	e7-e5
2	Ng1-f3	Ng8-f6
3	Nf3xe5	Nf6xe4?

Black is wrong to recapture im-

mediately, because it is White who
is able to make use of the open e-
file. A better plan for Black is
3 . . . d7-d6 4 Ne5-f3 Nf6xe4.

4 Qd1-e2

The white queen takes up station on the e-file.

4 ...   d7-d5

5 d2-d3   Ne4-f6

6 Ne5-c6+   Black resigns

White's double attack costs Black his queen. The knight has moved from e5 to attack the black queen, and Black cannot take him because the knight has also uncovered check from the white queen along the open e-file.

The queen is the most obvious target for a double attack, but sometimes White finds other black pieces to aim at:

Example 2—Game 33

(*Ruy López*)

1	e2-e4	e7-e5	**7 ...**	Qd8-d5
2	Ng1-f3	Nb8-c6	**8 d2-d3**	Ne4-f6
3	Bf1-b5	a7-a6	**9 Ne5-g6+**	Black resigns
4	Bb5xc6	d7xc6		

5 0-0

White can't win a pawn straight away: 5 Nf3xe5 Qd8-d4.

5 ...   Ng8-f6

6 Nf3xe5   Nf6xe4

Now the e-file is open and Black's problems begin.

7 Rf1-e1

Having castled safely, White seizes the opportunity to put his rook on the e-file.

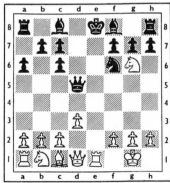

Once again the knight is involved in a double attack; the black rook is threatened in its corner, while check is discovered along the open e-file.

THE PIN

The idea here is very simple: you tempt your opponent to place a piece on the open e-file, pin it against his king, and attack it, usually with a pawn. The piece, pinned and unable to escape, is lost.

Of course, if you can tempt the enemy queen onto the open file, so much the better.

Example 1—Game 34

(Ruy López)

1	e2-e4	e7-e5
2	Ng1-f3	Nb8-c6
3	Bf1-b5	a7-a6
4	Bb5xc6	d7xc6
5	0-0	Ng8-f6
6	Nf3xe5	Qd8-d4
7	Ne5-f3	

Black is a pawn down, and his queen is attacked. He thinks he has the answer to his problems . . .

7	. . .	Qd4xe4
8	Rf1-e1	**Black resigns**

Catastrophe! In regaining his pawn, Black has lost his queen! The white rook has levelled its fire down the e-file, and scored a bulls eye with its first shot.

Catching the queen in this way is excellent, but a knight is the more usual target.

Example 2—Game 35

(Ruy López)

1	e2-e4	e7-e5
2	Ng1-f3	Nb8-c6
3	Bf1-b5	Bf8-c5
4	0-0	Ng8-f6
5	c2-c3	Nf6xe4

With his own king still in the centre, and a white rook itching to come to e1, Black is taking a chance in opening the e-file. 5 . . . 0-0 is a good alternative.

6 d2-d4   e5xd4

Another risky move. White would have had much the better game after 6 . . . Bc5-b6 7 Rf1-e1, but Black might have found time to get his king out of the centre before White opened fire.

7 Nf3xd4   Nc6xd4

8 c3xd4   Bc5-b4

The bishop stops the white rook from going to e1 immediately, but White can soon deal with that problem.

9 a2-a3   Bb4-a5

10 b2-b4

Bang goes Black's attack on e1!

10 . . .   Ba5-b6

11 Rf1-e1

The fatal pin!

11 . . .   f7-f5

12 f2-f3   Black resigns

Unable to move, the knight is doomed. Black has only two pawns for his piece, and has paid the penalty for leaving his king on the open e-file.

In all four examples White set a trap, and Black kindly walked straight into it. An open e-file is a source of danger, but if you are sensible and careful, if you think about what you are doing, and realize that there may be a trap, then nothing will happen to you. Always follow the two rules; get your king out of the centre, and put a rook on the e-file. Then you will be perfectly safe.

SUMMARY

A game of chess starts with both sides equal; if both sides play perfect moves the game must remain equal and end as a draw. You should never lose a game in the first few moves; if you do so then you must have made a big mistake in the opening. Follow the rules of opening play: develop your pieces, fight for the centre, don't waste time with unnecessary pawn moves or by moving the same piece twice. Always think carefully, and remember the two common danger areas are f7 and an open e-file.

Unless your opponent handles the opening very badly, you will rarely get the chance to start a king attack before the middle game. Sometimes the enemy king can be drawn out into the open, and this will give you the opportunity you are waiting for. Then you must begin your attack forcefully, but above all else bring your undeveloped pieces out into play as quickly as possible. Obviously if you are given the chance to attack you must do so; but your first job in a game of chess is to develop your pieces. Only when each of your men is placed on a good square can you really expect to be able to start a king attack.

7 Catching the king in the centre

If you can, stop your opponent from castling; tie his king down to the centre of the board and keep him there. When his king is stuck in the centre you gain three advantages.

(a) The enemy king will not have the protection of a strong pawn shield, and will therefore be easier to attack.

(b) The enemy rooks will not be able to get into the game along the central files.

(c) Your pieces—if you have developed properly—will be well-placed to attack in the centre.

Straight away we can lay down three rules for the attack:

(1) Open the central files for your rooks; in particular open the e-file.

(2) Use the weak point, f7, as a target.

(3) Remove—exchange or drive away—well-placed enemy defenders.

Look at Game 36 and see how Black follows these rules.

Game 36

(*English Opening*)

1	c2-c4	e7-e5
2	Nb1-c3	Ng8-f6
3	e2-e3	Bf8-c5
4	Ng1-f3	e5-e4
5	Nf3-d4	0-0

Black puts his king safely behind the barrier of pawns. At the same time he prepares to bring his rook into action along the e-file.

6	a2-a3	Bc5xd4
7	e3xd4	Nb8-c6
8	d4-d5	Nc6-e5

White has wasted time with too many pawn moves and Black has gained a lead in development. Now it is important for White to play 9 Bf1-e2 and castle quickly; instead he thinks he can win a pawn . . .

9	Qd1-c2	Rf8-e8!

. . . but he can't!

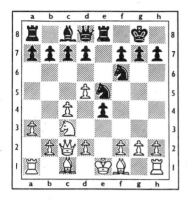

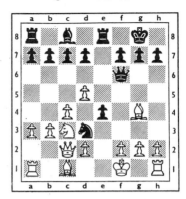

13   Be2xg4   Qe7-f6

The black rook has come to the e-file with immediate effect. If 10 Nc3xe4 Nf6xe4 11 Qc2xe4 Ne5-d3+ and the white queen is nailed to her king.

10   Bf1-e2   Ne5-d3+

11   Ke1-f1

Black's attacking power along the e-file has forced White to give up the right to castle: 11 Be2xd3 e4xd3 would have discovered check and won the white queen.

11   . . .   Qd8-e7

Black strengthens his power on the e-file, and defends his e-pawn. Now if 12 Be2xd3 e4xd3 13 Qc2xd3 Qe7-e1 is mate.

12   b2-b3   Nf6-g4

So far Black has played very sensibly; he has a small lead in development and has caught the white king in the centre. Now he attacks the weak point f2, but he breaks an important rule of the opening. Black is beginning to attack before all his pieces are in play. Can he afford to do this, or should he have developed his Q-side first?

The black rook can handle the e-file alone, so the queen puts f2 under the hammer.

14   Bg4-f3

The only other ways of stopping mate lose immediately: (a) 14 Nc3-d1 Qf6xa1, and (b) 14 f2-f3 Qf6-d4.

14   . . .   Qf6-d4

f2 is really under seige; there is yet another threat of mate, and White's reply is forced.

15   Nc3-d1

Black can win a rook by 15 . . . Qd4xa1, but he is much more interested in the white king. White has two active defenders, his king's bishop and his knight; they must be removed.

15   . . .   e4xf3

Now the e-file is open Black threatens mate on e1.

16   g2xf3   Re8-e1+

The rook's fuse has been smouldering for several moves. At last his chance has come and he scorches down the e-file to explode with devastating effect on e1.

| **17** | **Kf1-g2** | **Re1xd1** |

The final demolition!

White's knight, his last active defender, is removed, and with him goes White's support of f2.

| **18** | **Rh1xd1** | **Qd4xf2+** |

| **19** | **Kg2-h1** | |

Or 19 Kg2-h3 d7-d6 mate.

| **19** | **...** | **Nd3-f4** |

| **20** | **d2-d4** | |

Or 20 Rd1-g1 Qf2xf3+ 21 Rg1-g2 Qf3xg2 mate. White offers his queen in a desperate attempt to stave off mate, but Black isn't the least bit interested.

| **20** | **...** | **Qf2xf3+** |

| **21** | **Kh1-g1** | **Nf4-h3 mate** |

Black followed all our rules perfectly. He used the e-file as a highway into White's position, and f2 as a target for attack. He seized his chance to remove White's well-placed defenders and left the white king completely defenceless. Then it was a simple job for his queen and knight to finish off the good work.

As you can see, catching your opponent's king in the centre is well worth while. In fact it is so worth while that you should always be on the lookout for the possibility of sacrificing a pawn or even a piece just to keep him there.

In Game 36 Black did not have to sacrifice to trap his opponent's king in the centre, but he did break an important rule of development. Black's assault really began when he played 12 . . . Nf6-g4, and at that time his Q-side was undeveloped. Sometimes we must break rules. Sometimes rules contradict each other. Here the rules for attack were more important than the rules for development. The most important thing when your opponent's king is stuck in the centre is *TIME*. Your opponent must not be given the time to find a safe place for his king; he must not have the time to complete his development. You must keep him fully occupied by making him defend against your threats, and if you can at the same time bring more pieces into your attack then you must not miss the chance to do so. If you fail to follow your attack vigorously, if you give your opponent time, he may sort out his problems, he may get his pieces into play and gain a lead in development. Then it will be you who will have to pay the price for failing to develop properly.

We can now make two more rules. Most attacks on the enemy's uncastled king will begin before all your pieces are properly in play, so:

(4) Make sure that you keep more pieces in the attack than your opponent can bring to the defence.

(5) Keep your opponent busy, and do not give him time to sort out his problems.

We now have five rules. Obviously we cannot follow all of them every time, but as we shall see in the remaining games in this chapter, a successful attack on a king in the centre is always based upon them.

HOW TO CATCH THE KING IN THE CENTRE

There are four common reasons why a king cannot castle.

(a) You have made him move.

(b) His own pieces are in the way.

(c) You attack the square over which he must cross.

(d) You tie him to one of his own defenders.

We shall look at each one in turn, learn how to catch the king in the centre, and see how our five rules apply in the attack.

THE KING HAS HAD TO MOVE

This is obviously the simplest case for your attack; since your opponent's king has moved you don't have to worry about his ever finding a way to castle.

Game 37

(Caro-Kann Defence)

1	e2-e4	c7-c6
2	d2-d4	d7-d5
3	e4xd5	c6xd5
4	c2-c4	Ng8-f6
5	Nb1-c3	e7-e6
6	Ng1-f3	Bf8-e7
7	Bc1-f4	b7-b6

Black had cleared the way for castling and should have taken the chance to do so.

8 Nf3-e5

The knight takes a fine outpost, and fixes his eye on f7.

8	...	Bc8-b7
9	c4xd5	Nf6xd5
10	Bf1-b5+	

Now Black has to pay the price for his failure to castle; he cannot put

a piece in the way without it being taken, so he must move his king.

10 ... Ke8-f8

11 Qd1-h5

White begins the attack before he has castled himself. He can see that his king is perfectly safe where it is, and that he would be able to castle at the first sign of danger. Furthermore, pawns stand firm on both the e- and d-files, so there is no immediate attacking future for his rooks in the centre.

11 ... g7-g6

12 Qh5-f3

Black has beaten off the first mate threat and must not be given time to find a safe place for his king, so White renews his attack on f7 and threatens mate in two, beginning with 13 Bf4-h6+.

12 ... Be7-f6

Black blocks the f-file, but White has f7 firmly in his sights and is not going to be easily put off. The position of the black king only makes the problem greater: a black rook cannot come to f8 to cover f7.

13 Bf4-g5

Yet another threat. Black can't play 13 ... Bf6xg5 because of 14 Qf3xf7; so he must defend his bishop.

13 ... Kf8-g7

14   Bg5-h6+

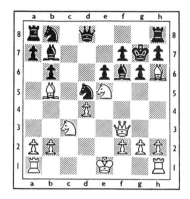

White keeps plugging away; Black is never given a moment's rest.

14   . . .   Kg7-g8
If 14 . . . Kg7xh6 15 Ne5xf7+ wins the black queen.

15   Bb5-e8!
The black f-pawn is in trouble again. White threatens 16 Be8xf7 mate.

15   . . .   Qd8xe8
Black has been on the rack as White has stuck firmly to rules 4 and 5—keeping him busy, never giving him a moment's peace, preventing him from getting his pieces into play —and all the time f7 has been under the hammer. White still has an advantage in development, and his pieces are placed for the final break-through.

16   Nc3xd5
The immediate task is to remove Black's active defenders and leave his king defenceless. Black's queen has already been lured away from f6, and now his knight and bishop face the firing squad.

16   . . .   Bf6xe5
Or 16 . . . Bb7xd5 17 Qf3xf6.

17   Nd5-f6+   Be5xf6

18   Qf3xf6
Now the target has switched from f7 to g7.

18   . . .   Black resigns

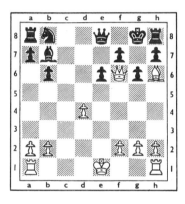

If he avoids the mate by 18 . . . Qe8-f8, then 19 Bh6xf8 Kg8xf8 20 Qf6xh8+, and Black is miles behind on material.

White made eight moves after forcing Black to move his king. Every single one of those eight moves contained a threat. The square f7 was the main target, and White's plan was to keep Black fully occupied, so tied up that he never had time to develop his Q-side, or find safety for his king.

In Game 37 the attacker's task was easy because his opponent's king had moved; there was never any fear of his suddenly castling into safety. When the king has not moved, the attacker, as well as trying to get at him, also has to make sure he stays in the centre.

CASTLING IS PREVENTED BY LACK OF DEVELOPMENT

In this case your opponent is unable to castle because his own pieces are in the way. You must continue to follow all the rules; but in particular you must make it as difficult as possible for your opponent to complete his development, by keeping him fully occupied defending against your threats.

Game 38

(Queen's Pawn Game)

1	d2-d4	Ng8-f6		
2	Nb1-c3	d7-d5		
3	Bc1-g5	c7-c5		
4	Ng1-f3	Nb8-c6		
5	Bg5xf6	e7xf6		
6	e2-e3	c5xd4		
7	Nf3xd4			

7	...	Bf8-b4
8	Nd4-e2	

White prevents his Q-side pawns from being split, but he wastes valuable development time.

8	...	0-0
9	a2-a3	Bb4xc3+
10	Ne2xc3	d5-d4!

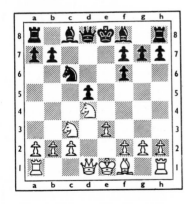

Black's pawn formation has been shattered, but he has free diagonals for his bishops, and his rook will soon be busily at work along the e-file.

Black, realizing he has a chance to catch the white king in the middle, smashes open the centre files.

11	e3xd4	Rf8-e8+

12   Nc3-e2

White wants to support his d-pawn with c2-c3, but he really should have taken the chance to complete his development with 12 Bf1-e2 and 13 0-0.

12   . . .   Qd8-b6

Black finds a new target, b2, and warns his opponent against castling Q-side.

13   c2-c3

With his king stuck in the centre White must support his d-pawn and keep the d-file closed to the black rooks.

13   . . .   Qb6xb2

14   Qd1-c1   Qb2-b5

15   Qc1-b1   Qb5-a5

16   Ke1-d1

White decides that it's high time he gave up any idea of castling. With his king on e1, both his knight and his c-pawn are pinned, Black threatens . . . Nc6xd4 and . . . Qa5xc3+, and White hasn't a hope of getting his K-side developed.

16   . . .   Bc8-f5

17   Qb1-b3

If 17 Qb1xb7 Qa5-a4+ and the white king is driven back to e1: 18 Kd1-d2 Qa4-c2+.

17   . . .   Ra8-d8

Black completes his development by bringing his rook to face the white king.

18   Kd1-c1

Even now White cannot get his K-side developed: 18 Ne2-g3 Nc6xd4 19 c3xd4 Re8-e1 mate.

Every one of Black's pieces is waiting, ready for the kill. The white king is protected from the full blast of Black's rooks only by the flimsy pawn barrier. Black sweeps the barrier aside.

18   . . .   Nc6xd4!!

The centre files are smashed open so that the black rooks can seize the white king by the scruff of his neck.

19   c3xd4

If 19 Ne2xd4 Rd8xd4   20 c3xd4 Re8-e1+   21 Kc1-b2 Qa5-d2+, and mate next move.

19	...	Qa5-e1+	

20 Qb3-d1 Rd8-c8+

The black rooks make full use of the open files.

21 Kc1-b2 Re8xe2+!

The white knight defends against a check on c3, and must be removed.

22 Bf1xe2

Or 22 Qd1xe2 Qe1-c3+ 23 Kb2-a2 Bf5-e6+ 24 Ka2-b1 Qc3-c1 mate.

22 ...   Qe1-c3+

23 Kb2-a2 Bf5-c2

24 Ra1-c1 Qc3-b3+

25 Ka2-a1 Qb3xa3 mate

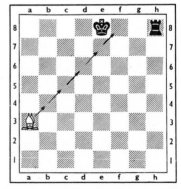

White fell behind in development and couldn't get his king out of the centre; Black made sure he stayed there by keeping White's pieces tangled. The finish was straightforward; Black smashed open the centre files and there was the white king, ready and waiting to be mated.

THE KING'S CROSSING SQUARE IS ATTACKED

In this case your opponent cannot castle because his king is unable to cross the f-file or the d-file.

Normally it is a rook on the d-file or a bishop attacking f8 that causes the trouble.

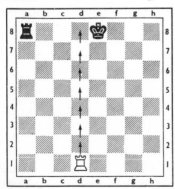

Black is unable to castle because his king cannot cross d8.

Black is unable to castle because his king cannot cross f8.

The rules for attacking are exactly the same. You must remember that, given time, your opponent may find a way to castle; so keep him fully occupied. Your opponent will probably try to close your line of attack so that he can castle. When a knight attacks the crossing square, there is no way of blocking it.

Game 39

(Scotch Game)

1	e2-e4	e7-e5
2	Ng1-f3	Nb8-c6
3	d2-d4	e5xd4
4	Bf1-c4	Ng8-f6
5	0-0	d7-d5?

Black is quite right to fight for the centre; . . . d7-d5 is a splendid move to aim for. However, in this position Black has made a really dreadful mistake; he is allowing the e-file to be opened when White has a rook bursting to come to e1, and his own king is not in a position to castle.

6	e4xd5	Nf6xd5
7	Nf3-g5	

Threatening 8 Ng5xf7, and making room for the queen to come to f3 or h5.

7	. . .	Bc8-e6
8	Rf1-e1	

Once again the e-file and f7 figure foremost in White's mind.

8	. . .	Bf8-e7
9	Re1xe6!	

With two black bishops on the e-file, White's rook was battering against a brick wall. Now the wall crumbles, and White's minor pieces invade.

9	. . .	f7xe6
10	Ng5xe6	

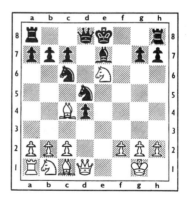

The first point of White's rook sacrifice: the black king is to be fixed in the centre. As long as White can keep his knight on e6 the black king will not be able to cross either d8 or f8; so castling will be impossible.

10 . . .   Qd8-d6

11   Bc4xd5

The second point: if 11 . . . Qd6xd5
12 Ne6xc7+, and Black's queen is
lost.

11   . . .   Be7-f6

12   Bc1-f4

White has a material advantage and
the black king is trapped in the
centre; he must now develop his
Q-side as quickly as possible. By
developing the bishop with a threat
he gives Black no time to find a
way to castle.

12   . . .   Nc6-e5

13   Nb1-d2

Again developing with a threat;
White plans 14 Nd2-c4 winning the
black knight.

13   . . .   Ke8-d7

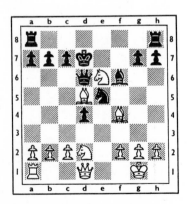

Black gives up hope of castling. He
defends c7 and can answer 14 Nd2-
c4 with 14 . . . Qd6xd5, but his
king is still not safe.

14   Bd5-b3

Again there is a threat: 15 Nd2-c4
Qd6-d5   16 Nc4xe5+, winning the
black queen.

14   . . .   Qd6-c6

15   Ne6xd4   Qc6-c5

The black queen is wandering aim-
lessly. White shunts her off into a
corner and then turns his attention
to the defenceless black king.

16   Nd2-e4   Qc5-b6

There is nothing better: (a) 16 . . .
Qc5-f8   17 Nd4-e6+ and (b) 16 . . .
Qc5-e7   17 Nd4-f5+ both cost
Black his queen, while (c) 16 . . .
Qc5-a5 is similar to the game.

17   Bf4xe5

With a big advantage in fire-power
White removes one of Black's last
active defenders.

17   . . .   Bf6xe5

18   Nd4-c6+

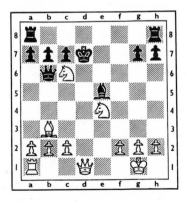

White rounds up the king. If 18
. . . Kd7xc6   19 Qd1-d5 is mate.

18	. . .	Kd7-e8
19	Qd1-h5+	g7-g6
20	Qh5xe5+	Ke8-f8
21	Qe5-e7 mate	

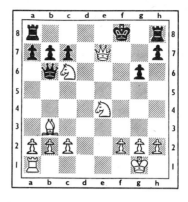

If Game 27 was Bronstein's 'dream game', then Game 39 must have been Black's 'knightmare'. The white knights created absolute havoc; the king's knight in particular had a field day, first on e6, trapping the king in the centre, and then on c6, keeping the queen out—and helping with the mating net.

THE KING HAS TO REMAIN IN THE CENTRE TO DEFEND ONE OF HIS OWN PIECES

There are two common cases:

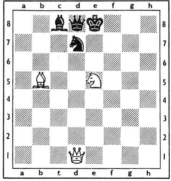

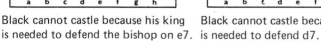

Black cannot castle because his king is needed to defend the bishop on e7.

Black cannot castle because his king is needed to defend d7.

Catching the king in the centre

When your opponent's king is held in the centre in this way, you must apply as much pressure as possible to the square he is having to defend. Attack it; try to remove its defenders; in that way you will keep the king tied in the middle. Your opponent must try to over-protect his danger point, and close your lines of attack by putting his pieces in the way. Then he will be able to castle and bring a rook to the centre.

Game 40

(Giuoco Piano)

1	e2-e4	e7-e5
2	Ng1-f3	Nb8-c6
3	Bf1-c4	Bf8-c5
4	c2-c3	Ng8-f6
5	d2-d4	e5xd4
6	c3xd4	Bc5-b4+
7	Nb1-c3	d7-d5
8	e4xd5	Nf6xd5
9	0-0	

White puts his own king into safety, and by attacking the black knight on d5 he denies Black the time to castle.

9 ...   Bc8-e6

Much better than 9 ... Nd5xc3 10 b2xc3 Bb4xc3 11 Bc1-a3, when White gladly gives up the exchange to trap the black king firmly in the centre.

10	Bc1-g5	Bb4-e7
11	Bc4xd5	

If White is to catch the black king in the centre he must first clear away some of the defensive pieces; then his rook can come to e1 with great effect.

11	...	Be6xd5
12	Nc3xd5	Qd8xd5
13	Bg5xe7	Nc6xe7
14	Rf1-e1	

Now the air has cleared and White has control of the e-file. Black cannot castle because his king is needed to defend his knight; he cannot block the white rook along the e-file, and if 14 ... Qd5-d7, White simply increases the pressure with 15 Qd1-e2.

14 ...   f7-f6

Black intends to play 15 . . . Ke8-f7, 16 . . . Rh8-e8, and 17 . . . Kf7-g8, when he will have 'castled'. White has other plans for the black king!

15   Qd1-e2   Qd5-d7

16   Ra1-c1   c7-c6

After this Black is doomed; he should have been more concerned with the safety of his king.

17   d4-d5!

White seizes his chance to smash open more lines.

17   ...   c6xd5

18   Nf3-d4   Ke8-f7

Black breaks the pin, but even now his king is tied to defending the knight.

19   Nd4-e6

White threatens to invade with the rook on c7.

19   ...   Rh8-c8

20   Qe2-g4   g7-g6

21   Ne6-g5+

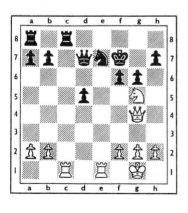

The black queen is en prise, so the king is forced back to e8.

21   ...   Kf7-e8

22   Re1xe7+!

The breakthrough almost inevitably comes down the e-file.

22   ...   Ke8-f8

Not (a) 22 . . . Qd7xe7 23 Rc1xc8+, or (b) 22 . . . Ke8xe7 23 Rc1-e1+ Ke7-d6 24 Qg4-b4+ Kd6-c7 25 Ng5-e6+ Kc7-b8 26 Qb4-f4+.

23   Re7-f7+   Kf8-g8

24   Rf7-g7+   Kg8-h8

The wretched rook can't be taken: (a) 24 . . . Kg8xg7 25 Qg4xd7+, and (b) 24 . . . Qd7xg7 25 Rc1xc8+. The black king is now finished off rapidly.

25   Rg7xh7+   Kh8-g8

26   Rh7-g7+   Kg8-h8

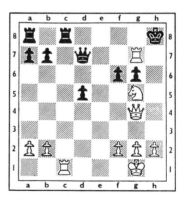

Or 26 . . . Kg8-f8 27 Ng5-h7+.

27   Qg4-h4+   Kh8xg7

28   Qh4-h7+   Kg7-f8

29	Qh7-h8+	Kf8-e7
30	Qh8-g7+	Ke7-e8
31	Qg7-g8+	Ke8-e7
32	Qg8-f7+	Ke7-d8
33	Qf7-f8+	Qd7-e8
34	Ng5-f7+	Kd8-d7
35	Qf8-d6 mate	

Black lost because his king was held in the centre, defending e7, for too long. Even when he had moved his king to f7 White's pressure was fierce, and it was no surprise when the rook sacrifice broke through on the e-file.

Before the end of this chapter, two small warnings.

BEWARE ARTIFICIAL CASTLING

In Game 40 Black, unable to castle by the normal method, tried to get his king to g8 by moving his king and rook separately. This is called artificial castling. In fact Black was unable to castle artificially either, but it is a possibility you should keep in mind. If your opponent finds an easy method of castling artificially you may have wasted time chasing his king.

Example

1	e2-e4	e7-e5
2	Ng1-f3	Nb8-c6
3	Bf1-c4	Ng8-f6
4	0-0	Bf8-e7
5	Nb1-c3	Nf6xe4

If now 6 Nc3xe4, Black regains his piece with 6 . . . d7-d5.

6	Bc4xf7+	Ke8xf7
7	Nc3xe4	

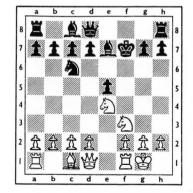

Catching the king in the centre

White has achieved his aim; the
material is level, and the black king
has had to move. However, White's
pieces are not in a position to follow
up the attack and Black can castle
artificially.

7	...	d7-d5
8	Ne4-g3	Rh8-f8
9	d2-d3	Kf7-g8

Now Black has 'castled' and actually
has the advantage, because of his
strong pawn centre and extra space.

Before setting off on a time-consuming series of moves aimed at making the
king give up castling, make sure that he cannot simply castle artificially.
Make sure that you are not wasting moves driving the enemy to safety!

BEWARE THE QUEEN EXCHANGE

When the d-file is opened early and the queens are exchanged, often the
king has to recapture.

Example

1	e2-e4	e7-e5
2	d2-d4	d7-d6
3	d4xe5	d6xe5
4	Qd1xd8	Ke8xd8

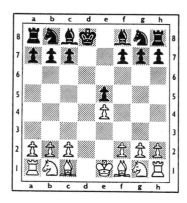

Here White has gained almost nothing by making the king move. Without
his queen White will find it difficult to build up a king attack; he simply
won't have the fire-power. In these circumstances it doesn't matter if

Black has to waste a little time. Black will probably play . . . c7-c6—a good move since it attacks d5—and then . . . Kd8-c7, when his king will be perfectly safe and out of the way.

With the queens on the board your attacking power is greater; with the queens exchanged castling is unimportant, since the king is less likely to have to meet a direct attack. Don't be tempted to exchange queens in the opening *simply* to prevent your opponent from castling.

SUMMARY

Catch the king in the centre if you can. Be prepared to sacrifice if necessary, to keep the king where you want him. Then, get at him! Use f7 as a target, and batter open the centre files for your rooks. Never give your opponent time to take breath; keep pressing forward; keep him busy. Time is important; you need it to bring your pieces into battle. Your opponent must not have it, or he will solve his problems of development.

8 Attacking the castled king

The castled king hides in a fortress. In front of him a sturdy line of pawns stand on sentry duty, a rook patrols the rank and defends his side, and a knight is the advance guard to warn away the enemy attackers.

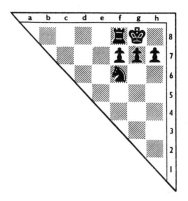

Normal castled position showing Black's regiment of defenders.

Your task is to smash your way into the fortress and lay open the enemy king. Of course, you should always be on the look-out for a snap mate, but power is the real key to unlocking the fortress. You must follow the rules we laid down in chapter three, and steadily increase your fire-power, until the enemy defences crack under the weight of your attackers. Try to control the centre; gain an advantage in space, and your pieces will have plenty of room to move around. Then you will find it easy to switch them from the centre to the wings, and begin an attack upon the castled position.

Look at Game 41 and see how White builds and carries out his attack:

Game 41

(French Defence)

1	e2-e4	e7-e6
2	d2-d4	d7-d5
3	Nb1-c3	d5xe4
4	Nc3xe4	

Black has played a quiet defence and White, with a strong centre pawn on d4 against a backward black pawn on e6, has a small advantage in space.

4	...	Nb8-d7
5	Ng1-f3	Ng8-f6
6	Ne4xf6+	Nd7xf6
7	Bf1-d3	Bf8-e7
8	0-0	0-0
9	Qd1-e2	b7-b6
10	Bc1-g5	

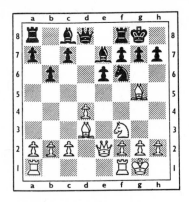

Clearly the white pieces have more room, but before he can switch to a K-side attack White must take a firm grip on the centre. Black must counter in the centre to free his position quickly by playing ... c7-c5; so White tries to hold up this move for as long as possible.

10 ...   Bc8-b7
Not 10 ... c7-c5   11 Bg5xf6 Be7xf6   12 Qe2-e4, forking the rook on a8 and mate on h7.

11 Ra1-d1
Now 11 ... c7-c5   12 d4xc5 Be7xc5   13 Bd3xh7+ costs Black his queen, so he removes her from the d-file.

11 ...   Qd8-c8

12 c2-c4
Again White keeps Black tied up. If 12 ... c7-c5   13 d4-d5 and Black's e-pawn is pinned; so now he defends his bishop.

12 ...   Rf8-e8

13 Nf3-e5
White steadily increases his hold on the centre.

Now 13 ... c7-c5   14 Bg5xf6 Be7xf6   15 Bd3xh7+ Kg8xh7 16 Qe2-h5+ Kh7-g8   17 Qh5xf7+ Kg8-h7   18 Rd1-d3 leads to mate.

13 ...   h7-h6
Black gets rid of the annoying bishop, but at the cost of breaking his line of sentry pawns.

14 Bg5-d2   c7-c5
At last!

15 Bd2-c3   c5xd4

16 Bc3xd4   Qc8-c7

17 Bd4-c3   Ra8-d8

18 Rf1-e1

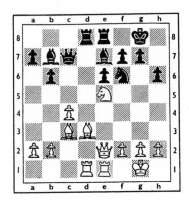

The first stage of White's plan is at an end, and his army makes a fine sight. The knight spearheads the troops, the heavy pieces pound away down the middle, and the bishops rake through the centre onto Black's castled position.

18	...	Bb7-a8
19	Qe2-e3	Qc7-b7
20	Qe3-h3	

White answers the threat of 20 ... Qb7xg2 mate, and begins the second stage of his plan: to switch his fire-power to the K-side.

20	...	Be7-c5
21	b2-b4	Bc5-f8

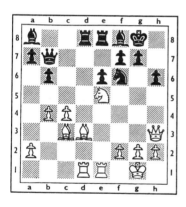

White wants to transfer his rook from e1 to g3, but the immediate 22 Re1-e3 is met by 22 ... Nf6-e4! Throughout the second stage of White's plan he must be careful that he does not commit so much of his power to the K-side that he leaves himself wide open for a counter-attack in the centre.

22	Rd1-d2	Qb7-e7

23	Re1-e3	Ba8-b7

The white pieces have such a stranglehold on the centre that Black simply cannot find a sensible plan.

24	Rd2-e2	Nf6-h7

To answer 25 Re3-g3 with 25 ... Nh7-g5.

25	f2-f4	f7-f6

Another of the sentry pawns advances, and White can see daylight around the black king.

26	Ne5-g4	Qe7-c7
27	Re3-g3	

The second stage of White's plan is complete; he has switched his pieces to the K-side without allowing Black any chance to counter in the centre.

27	...	Kg8-h8

Or 27 ... Qc7xf4 28 Ng4xh6+ Kg8-h8 29 Nh6-f7+.

28 Bd3xh7!

The third and final stage of White's plan is to dynamite the castled position; blow the defences sky high, and seize the enemy king. White begins by removing the black knight.

28	...	Rd8-d1+
29	Re2-e1	Rd1xe1+
30	Bc3xe1	Kh8xh7

Black's play in the centre has forced exchanges and cut down White's army, but there is no stopping the remaining white attackers.

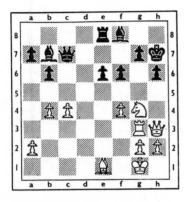

31 Qh3xh6+!!
A brilliant breakthrough. If 31 . . . g7xh6 32 Ng4xf6+ Kh7-h8 33 Rg3-g8 mate.

31	...	Kh7-g8

32 Ng4xf6+
Black's defences are completely wrecked and White finishes the job rapidly.

32	...	Kg8-f7
33	Qh6-g6+	Kf7-e7
34	Qg6xe8+	Ke7xf6

Or 34 . . . Ke7-d6 35 Rg3-d3+ Bb7-d5 36 Nf6-e4 mate.

35	Rg3-g6+	Kf6-f5
36	Qe8xe6+	Kf5xf4
37	Be1-d2 mate	

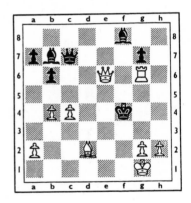

You should learn three lessons from this game:

(a) Get a firm grip on the centre.

(b) Switch your fire-power to the K-side and keep the centre under control.

(c) Dynamite the castled position and kill the king.

Now that the three stages of the plan are clear, we shall look at different ways of attacking.

STORMING THE CASTLED POSITION WITH PAWNS

A pawn attack is the simplest way of destroying the enemy defences. Pawns are cheap, and when one is exchanged or lost, a file is opened and all the pieces gain fire-power. In Game 42 Black's castled position crumbles under an avalanche of white pawns.

Game 42

(Benoni-Indian Defence)

1	d2-d4	Ng8-f6
2	c2-c4	e7-e6
3	Nb1-c3	c7-c5
4	d4-d5	e6xd5
5	c4xd5	d7-d6
6	e2-e4	Bf8-e7

There is not much future for the bishop on this square, so 6 . . . g7-g6 followed by 7 . . . Bf8-g7 would have been better.

7	Bf1-d3	0-0
8	Ng1-f3	Bc8-g4
9	h2-h3	Bg4-h5

The black pieces on the K-side are inviting the white pawns to advance.

10	g2-g4	Bh5-g6
11	0-0	Rf8-e8

12 Nf3-d2

White supports his e-pawn and clears the way for f2-f4-f5.

12	. . .	Nf6-d7
13	f2-f4	f7-f6

White has built a strong centre and Black is very cramped. The white pawns stand ready to demolish Black's castled position, but this will be of no use if the white pieces are unable to invade the ruins. White must first complete his development and group his pieces to support the break-through.

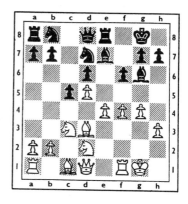

14	b2-b3	Nb8-a6
15	Bc1-b2	Na6-c7
16	Qd1-f3	Qd8-b8

Black has no chance of hitting back on the K-side or in the centre; so he tries for a counter-attack on the Q-side, and White must hold up this advance.

17	a2-a4	a7-a6
18	h3-h4	h7-h6
19	Qf3-h3	

Threatening 20 g4-g5 Nd7-f8 21 h4-h5 Bg6-f7 22 g5-g6 trapping the black bishop.

19	...	Nd7-f8
20	Rf1-f2	

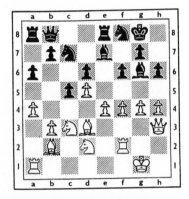

The first stage of the plan is over; White has the centre under control and his pieces developed and ready to meet Black's play on the Q-side. Now he prepares the switch to the K-side. His king's rook is ready to transfer to g2 or h2, and f1 is left open for his queen's rook.

20	...	b7-b6
21	Nc3-e2	

Heading for f4, and opening the line of the queen's bishop.

21	...	Qb8-c8
22	f4-f5	Bg6-f7

23	Nd2-f3	Nf8-h7
24	Ne2-f4	

As his pawns advance White finds space for his pieces to line up behind them.

24	...	b6-b5
25	a4-a5	

Now that his pieces are gathering for the breakthrough on the K-side, White doesn't want Black to get any sort of counter-play by opening files on the Q-side.

25	...	Qc8-b7
26	Bd3-c2	

Black was threatening 26 ... c5-c4; this is now simply answered by 27 b3-b4.

26	...	Re8-c8
27	Rf2-g2	Nc7-e8

End of stage two; White has switched his fire-power to the K-side, and is ready for the final push.

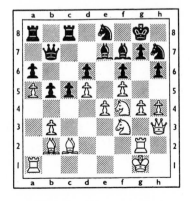

28 g4-g5!
The white pawns will smash open the castled position.

28	...	f6xg5
29	h4xg5	Nh7xg5
30	Nf3xg5	Be7xg5
31	Rg2xg5!	

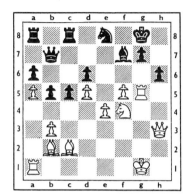

The white pawns have done their job, and the pieces invade.

31	...	h6xg5
32	Nf4-g6	

Threatening 33 Qh3-h8 mate.

32	...	Bf7xg6
33	f5xg6	Ne8-f6

34	Qh3-e6+	Kg8-f8

If 34 ... Kg8-h8 35 Kg1-g2, and 36 Ra1-h1 is deadly. Now White removes Black's last active defender and the game is all over.

35	Bb2xf6	g7xf6
36	Ra1-f1	Qc7-e7
37	g6-g7+	Qe7xg7
38	Rf1xf6+	Black resigns

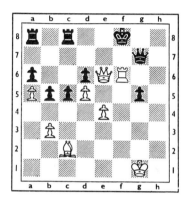

Black's queen is lost.

The story of White's attack is quite straightforward. He advanced his pawns and massed his pieces behind them, the pawns smashed open Black's defences, and the pieces poured in through the ruins to seize the king.

Although a pawn attack is the simplest way to drive away the enemy's defenders and shatter the pawn shield around his king, you won't often get the chance to carry out this sort of attack. Pawn attacks are slow. In the first few moves of your pawn attack you don't usually threaten anything; so your opponent has time to start a plan of his own in the centre or on the Q-side. If he breaks through first, then he will cut you in two, leaving your attacking pawns stranded up field, and your king naked behind them! Game 43 is a good example of just how dangerous it is to advance pawns in front of your own king.

Game 43

(Sicilian Defence—Dragon Variation)

1	e2-e4	c7-c5
2	Ng1-f3	d7-d6
3	d2-d4	c5xd4
4	Nf3xd4	Ng8-f6
5	Nb1-c3	g7-g6
6	f2-f4	Nb8-d7
7	Bf1-e2	Bf8-g7
8	Bc1-e3	0-0
9	0-0	a7-a6
10	a2-a4	Qd8-c7

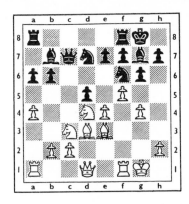

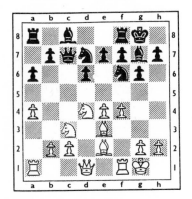

White now begins a pawn assault on the K-side; this plan is quite wrong because he does not have a firm enough hold on the centre, and Black is in a position to counter-attack.

11	f4-f5	b7-b6
12	g2-g4	Bc8-b7

White's pawn storm has got just as far as it is ever going. Black first attacks the white e-pawn and then smashes the centre wide open.

| 13 | Be2-d3 | d6-d5! |

14	e4xd5	Nf6xd5
15	Nc3xd5	Bb7xd5
16	c2-c3	

White's attack has ground to a halt and he tries to support his centre, but Black has scented blood. The white pawns on f5 and g4 are useless and their king lies open, wishing his sentries could return.

| 16 | ... | Bg7-e5 |

The black bishop comes into the centre and scythes behind White's pawns to hit h2.

| 17 | Rf1-f2 | Be5xh2+! |

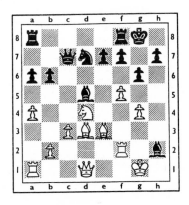

Attacking the castled king

All the sentry pawns are gone and White has only his pieces to defend his king against the onslaught.

18 Kg1-f1

Not 18 Rf2xh2 Qc7-g3+ 19 Kg1-f1 Qg3xh2.

18	...	Bh2-g3
19	Rf2-d2	Nd7-c5
20	Be3-h6	Nc5xd3
21	Rd2xd3	Bd5-c4
22	Bh6xf8	Qc7-f4+

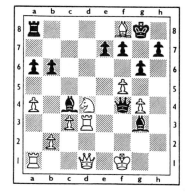

Black's pieces wander as they like behind White's pawns; it is only a matter of time before they catch up with the white king.

23	Nd4-f3	Ra8-d8
24	Kf1-g2	Rd8xd3
25	Qd1-e2	

White grimly defends his knight, but . . .

25 ... Rd3xf3!

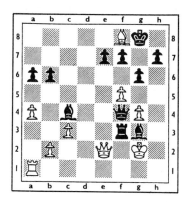

26	Qe2xf3	Bc4-d5!
27	Qf3xd5	Qf4-f2+
28	Kg2-h3	Qf2-h2 mate

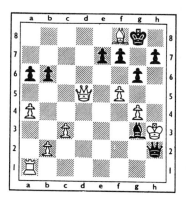

The black king has been rounded up behind his advanced pawns and executed.

White's pawn attack failed because he did not have a firm enough grip on the centre. The pawn moves f4-f5 and g2-g4 threatened absolutely nothing. If White had been allowed another two or three moves he might well have broken into Black's K-side and then it could have been a different story. But, White didn't have time. In fact, White's slow pawn advance gave Black the time he needed to counter-attack in the centre, and then White was far too busy trying to defend his king to have any further thoughts of attack.

A counter-attack in the centre is always the best answer to an attack on the side of the board. That is most important, so let's say it again in big letters: A COUNTER-ATTACK IN THE CENTRE IS ALWAYS THE BEST ANSWER TO AN ATTACK ON THE SIDE OF THE BOARD.

You cannot hope to carry out a successful pawn-storm if your opponent has a chance to counter-attack in the centre. Either you must control the centre completely or it must be hopelessly blocked. If the centre is completely blocked with pawns then the conditions should be perfect for your K-side pawn-storm. Look at Game 44.

Game 44

(French Defence)

1	e2-e4	e7-e6
2	d2-d4	d7-d5
3	Nb1-c3	Ng8-f6
4	Bc1-g5	Bf8-e7
5	e4-e5	Nf6-e4
6	Nc3xe4	Be7xg5
7	Ne4xg5	Qd8xg5

White has a small advantage in space due to his advanced e-pawn, but Black has avoided becoming too cramped by exchanging four of the minor pieces.

8	g2-g3	c7-c5
9	c2-c3	Nb8-c6
10	f2-f4	Qg5-e7
11	Ng1-f3	Bc8-d7
12	Qd1-d2	0-0
13	Bf1-d3	c5-c4

Black intends to attack on the Q-side, but by making this advance he takes the pressure away from d4 and frees all the white forces defending that square.

14　Bd3-c2

Of course the bishop remains lined up on h7.

14	...	b7-b5
15	0-0	a7-a5
16	Ra1-e1	b5-b4

White has already completed the first two stages of the attacking plan; he has a firm hold on the centre and more space on the K-side where his pieces are lined up to attack. White's problem is that two of his minor pieces have been exchanged, so his queen and rooks will have to do most of the attacking, and there are no open files for them to use.

17 f4-f5!

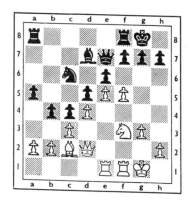

The chain of pawns across the middle of the board stops Black from counter-attacking in the centre, so it is perfectly safe for White to throw forward the pawns in front of his own king.

17	...	e6xf5

Black could not allow the white pawn to march on to f6.

18 g3-g4!

Open files are absolutely necessary for White's rooks. A couple of pawns will count for little if the rooks can build up their full firepower and pound into the enemy king's position.

18	...	f5xg4
19	Nf3-g5	g7-g6

If 19 ... h7-h6 20 Ng5-h7 Rf8-d8 21 Nh7-f6+! gives White a winning attack.

20 Rf1-f6

The white pawns have done their job by clearing the way for his pieces to sail into Black's K-side. The fact that White's own king is completely open doesn't matter at all; the centre files and diagonals are tightly shut; so the black pieces have no lines of attack.

20	...	Kg8-g7

Not 20 ... h7-h6 21 Bc2xg6 f7xg6 22 Rf6xg6+ Kg8-h8 23 Rg6xh6+ Kh8-g8 24 Rh6-g6+

Kg8-h8   25 e5-e6 Bd7-e8   26 Ng5-f7+, when White threatens 27 Qd2-h6 mate, and wins easily.

21   Re1-f1

Now the two rooks work together on the file, and f7 comes under seige.

21   . . .   Bd7-e8

22   Qd2-f4

White could have won the exchange with 22 Ng5-e6+, but he is after more. Just five moves after advancing his f-pawn White has all three heavy pieces pounding down the open file.

22   . . .   Nc6-d8

Black can only back-pedal and support f7.

23   e5-e6!

A marvellous move; attacking f7 yet again, and leaving e5 open for his queen. Black cannot capture, because his f-pawn is horribly pinned.

23   . . .   Ra8-a6

24   Qf4-e5!

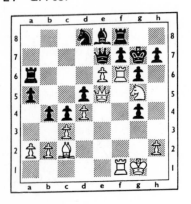

The queen signs Black's death warrant! Immediately White threatens 25 Rf6xg6 mate.

24   . . .   Kg7-h6

The black king had to escape from the white queen and, 24 . . . Kg7-g8 25 e6xf7+ would lose him his rook on a6.

25   Rf1-f5

The white rooks make full use of the f-file.

25   . . .   f7xe6

26   Ng5-f7+   Qe7xf7

Or 26 . . . Kh6-g7 27 Rf6xg6++ Kg7xg6   28 Rf5-f1 mate.

27   Rf5-h5+   Kh6-g7

28   Rf6xg6 mate

Advancing pawns in front of your own king is safe when the centre is blocked and your opponent has no hope of opening it. In this game White had to advance his pawns, because exchanging them was the only way he could get the open lines his pieces needed.

Be extremely careful before throwing pawns into a K-side attack. Piece attacks are always much quicker than pawn attacks. Make sure that your opponent cannot break open the centre or counter-attack rapidly on the Q-side. When you advance your K-side pawns you leave your own king naked; make sure the enemy pieces cannot get at him. If it is safe to advance your pawns, then hurl them forward, exchange them to open lines for your pieces, and use them to batter down the walls of the enemy fortress.

WEAKENING THE FORTRESS

If we can weaken the walls of a fortress, then obviously we shall find it easier to break in. The line of sentry pawns in front of the king form the wall of his fortress. When these three pawns stand in a line on their original squares, the fortress is strong and the king is safe.

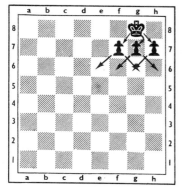

The strong fortress

The sentry pawns closely shield their king, and attack all the squares in front of them on the third rank, keeping the enemy at bay.

The king stands safely behind his sentries and defends each of them.

If any one of the pawns moves, the fortress becomes weaker. The king will no longer defend all the pawns. and he will not be so well shielded by them. At the same time the squares on the third rank will lose some of their cover, and become targets for the attacking pieces.

Your task as the attacker is clear: to weaken the fortress, make the sentry pawns move. Then your pieces will be able to move in through the gaps in the enemy defence. Also, you will find it much easier to destroy the pawn shield completely. Look at Game 45.

Game 45

(Colle System)

1	d2-d4	d7-d5
2	Ng1-f3	Ng8-f6
3	e2-e3	e7-e6
4	Bf1-d3	c7-c5
5	c2-c3	Nb8-c6
6	Nb1-d2	Bf8-e7
7	0-0	c5-c4?

On c5 the black pawn was attacking the white d-pawn. This advance to c4 throws away all the pressure on White's centre. White, who is planning to play e3-e4, will find that move easier to play now that his e-pawn is not needed to support d4.

8	Bd3-c2	b7-b5
9	e3-e4	d5xe4
10	Nd2xe4	0-0
11	Qd1-e2	

If Black is to challenge White for the centre, he must undermine the pawn on d4. This is difficult, because the black c-pawn has already advanced too far, and . . . e6-e5 is impossible because of White's control of e5. Already White is completing the first stage of the attacking plan; he has a firm enough grip on the centre to begin to think of switching to the K-side.

11 . . . Bc8-b7

Forced; White was threatening 12 Ne4xf6+ Be7xf6 13 Qe2-e4, forking h7 and c6.

12 Nf3-g5!

White begins stage two of his K-side attack and immediately forces Black to weaken his pawn shield. The threat is 13 Ne4xf6+ Be7xf6 14 Ng5xh7.

| 12 | ... | h7-h6 |

If 12 ... Nf6xe4 13 Qe2xe4, and Black is forced to move one of the pawns to prevent mate on h7.

| 13 | Ne4xf6+ | Be7xf6 |
| 14 | Qe2-e4! | |

Mate is threatened on h7, so another black pawn is forced to move.

| 14 | ... | g7-g6 |

The black castled position has been seriously weakened; the king has been separated from two of his pawns, and Black is losing control of his third rank. Everything is ready for the final stage of White's attack.

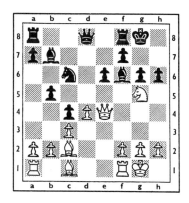

| 15 | | Ng5xe6! |

White seizes his chance to take the fortress walls apart, brick by brick! First the black f-pawn disappears ...

| 15 | ... | f7xe6 |
| 16 | Qe4xg6+ | |

... and then the g-pawn.

| 16 | ... | Bf6-g7 |
| 17 | Qg6-h7+ | |

White could have added the h-pawn to his collection by 17 Bc1xh6, but the black king is so open that White does not hesitate to push ahead with the attack.

| 17 | ... | Kg8-f7 |
| 18 | Bc2-g6+ | Kf7-f6 |

If 18 ... Kf7-e7, the white queen simply snaps up both the black bishops.

| 19 | Bg6-h5 | |

Threatening 20 Qh7-g6+, again winning the black bishops.

| 19 | ... | Nc6-e7 |

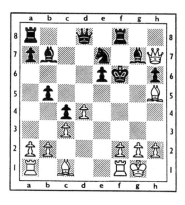

| 20 | Bc1xh6 | |

The last sentry falls, and White threatens 21 Qh7xg7+ Kf6-f5 22 Qg7-e5 mate. With his pawn shield entirely destroyed the black king cannot survive for long.

| 20 | ... | Rf8-g8 |
| 21 | h2-h4 | |

Threatening 22 Bh6-g5 mate.

21	...	e6-e5

If 21 ... Bg7xh6 22 Qh7-f7 mate.

22	Bh6xg7+	Rg8xg7
23	d4xe5+	Kf6xe5
24	Qh7xg7+	Black resigns

Black is way behind on pieces and his king is stranded, defenceless, in mid-board.

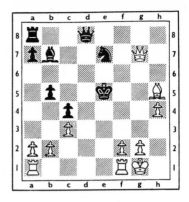

As the black sentry pawns advanced they lost the protection of their king, became weaker, and were targets for attack. At the same time the king himself lost the cover *they* should have given *him*. White swiftly destroyed the pawn shield, and with his fortress walls collapsing around him, the black king was a sitting duck; he never had a chance.

In Game 45 White weakened the black sentry pawns, and then demolished them. In the next game Black weakens White's pawn shield and then wriggles his pieces in through the gaps in the defence:

Game 46

(*Ruy López*)

1	e2-e4	e7-e5
2	Ng1-f3	Nb8-c6
3	Bf1-b5	f7-f5
4	d2-d4	f5xe4
5	Nf3xe5	

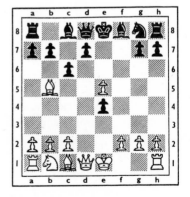

White threatens to catch the black king in the centre by 6 Qd1-h5+.

5	...	Nc6xe5
6	d4xe5	c7-c6!

A splendid move, attacking the bishop, opening a diagonal for the queen, and preparing to build a strong pawn centre.

7	Bb5-c4	Qd8-a5+
8	Nb1-c3	Qa5xe5
9	0-0	

White is a pawn down; so he tries to hurry his development and get a quick attack going. Yet, he would have done much better to have prepared for castling on the Q-side; on the king's wing he has no minor pieces to defend his fortress.

9	...	d7-d5
10	Bc4-b3	Ng8-f6
11	Bc1-e3	Bf8-d6

Black has such complete command of the centre that he is able to begin to build a K-side attack as he finishes his development. Immediately there is a threat of 12 ... Qe5xh2 mate; so White has to advance one of his sentry pawns.

12 g2-g3

The fortress has been weakened, and Black can see daylight around the white king.

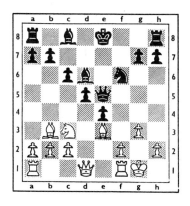

On g2 the white pawn was doing a useful job controlling f3 and h3. Now that it has moved, these two squares become weaker, and are targets for the black invaders.

12 ... Bc8-g4!

Straight away Black homes in on the weakened squares on White's K-side.

13 Qd1-d2 Bg4-f3

White has no control at all over f3; so he cannot kick out the black bishop which sits so comfortably in its hole in his fortress wall.

14 Be3-f4 Qe5-f5

White's weak points are all on the light squares, g2, h3, f3, and g4; so Black can well afford to give up his dark-squared bishop to bring his queen into battle.

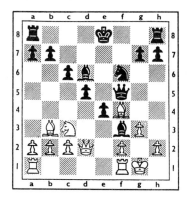

15 Nc3-d1

If 15 Bf4xd6 Qf5-h3, and White cannot stop mate on g2.

15 ... Qf5-h3

16 Nd1-e3

White prevents mate on g2, but ...

16 ...   **Nf6-g4**

. . . he is still being hammered on the light squares. Now mate is threatened on h2.

17   Rf1-c1

White can't defend h2, so he tries to make room for his king to flee.

17 ...   **Qh3xh2+**

18   Kg1-f1   **Qh2-h1 mate**

Total triumph for Black's invasion force! When White moved his g-pawn he lost control of f3 and h3. Black instantly grabbed his chance to attack on the light squares, and his pieces poured in through the holes in the fortress walls.

Sometimes your opponent will quite deliberately weaken his pawn shield by moving his g-pawn, right at the beginning of the game. This will be to fianchetto his bishop.

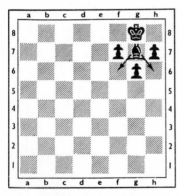

The fianchetto position

Black realizes that his pawn shield is weakened, but hopes that his bishop will be a strong defensive piece, since it stands next to the king and attacks both of the weak squares, h6 and f6.

If the centre is under control the attacker can storm the fianchetto position with his h-pawn or f-pawn, and open a file for his rook, but usually he will have to attack with his pieces. Look at Game 47.

Game 47

(*King's Indian Defence*)

1	d2-d4	Ng8-f6
2	c2-c4	g7-g6
3	Nb1-c3	Bf8-g7
4	e2-e4	d7-d6
5	f2-f4	

The Four Pawns Attack. White intends to throw his pawns forward in the centre, gain space, push his opponent's pieces to poor positions, and then switch to a K-side attack.

5	...	0-0
6	Ng1-f3	c7-c5

Of course, Black must challenge White's centre pawns.

7	d4-d5	e7-e6
8	Bf1-e2	e6xd5
9	e4-e5	

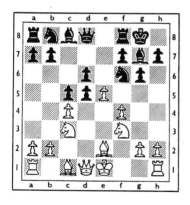

A risky and tricky idea. White wants to dislodge Black's knight from his K-side, though it may cost him a pawn.

9	...	d6xe5
10	f4xe5	Nf6-g4

11 Bc1-g5

White fires the first warning shot. Directly he attacks the black queen, but also he is beginning to eye f6.

Now Black has a problem. The safest square for his queen is a5, where she would also be out of the way of his undeveloped pieces. However, White is massing for an attack down the centre and on the K-side, and the queen would not be able to help in the defence from a5, so Black decides to leave her in the middle.

11	...	Qd8-d7
12	Nc3xd5	

The knight slips into the attack, and f6 really comes under the microscope.

12	...	Ng4xe5
13	Nf3xe5	Bg7xe5

All three black sentry pawns stand on light squares; so they only attack light squares. This means that Black's pieces must protect all the dark squares around his fortress. White must attack those dark squares and try to remove the black defenders. Already White has prised the black bishop from its defensive post on g7, now he cuts it off completely.

14 Bg5-f6!

The dark squares come under heavy fire; the black king is stuck without a move and White threatens 15 Nd5-e7+. To make matters worse Black can't even capture the wretched white bishop, for if 14 . . . Be5xf6 15 Nd5xf6+ forks king and queen.

14 . . .   Be5-d6

Not 14 . . . Nb8-c6 15 Bf6xe5 Nc6xe5 16 Nd5-f6+. Even though his dark-squared bishop is a fine attacking piece, White should always be prepared to exchange it for Black's dark-squared bishop. With the bishops gone, Black's weak dark squares become even weaker.

15 Qd1-d2!

Of course! The white queen develops straight onto a dark-squared diagonal, and threatens to thunder in on h6, and mate on g7.

15 . . .   Rf8-e8

Black must make room for his bishop to retreat to f8 to cover the weak squares g7 and h6.

16 Bf6-c3

Threatening murder by 17 Nd5-f6+!

16 . . .   Bd6-e7

The black bishop does its best, but there are far too many weak dark squares for him to cover.

17 Qd2-h6

Threatening mate on g7, and this time the black bishop simply can't cope: 17 . . . Be7-f8 18 Nd5-f6+ Kg8-h8 19 Qh6xh7 mate.

17 . . .   f7-f6

Black is forced to make another pawn move; his fortress becomes weaker, and his king draughtier.

18 0-0

After 18 Nd5xf6+ Be7xf6, or 18 Bc3xf6 Be7-f8, Black can cling on.

18 . . .   Nb8-c6

19 Rf1xf6!

One sentry less to deal with!

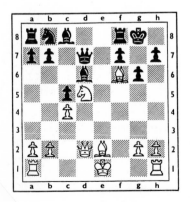

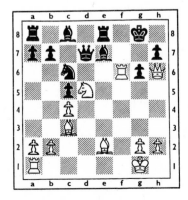

White threatens 20 Rf6xg6+ followed by 21 Qh6-g7 mate; he is wriggling his pieces into the fortress, closer and closer to the black king.

19 ...   Nc6-d4

Black just can't stomach White's dark-squared bishop slashing across the board at him any longer, so he cuts off the diagonal.

20   Be2-g4!   Qd7-d8

Taking the bishop would be equally disastrous: 20 . . . Qd7xg4   21 Nd5x e7+ and 22 Rf6-f8 mates.

21   Rf6-f7

This time mate is threatened on h7 as well as on g7.

21	**...**	**Kg8xf7**
22	**Qh6xh7+**	**Kf7-f8**

23	**Bc3xd4**	**c5xd4**
24	**Ra1-f1+**	**Black resigns**

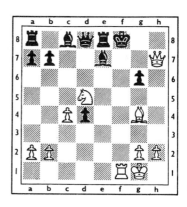

Black has to give up half his army to stop mate!

We have looked at two ways of taking advantage of pawn weaknesses in the enemy fortress.

(a) Destroy the weakened pawn shield.

(b) Wriggle pieces in through the holes in the pawn shield.

Attacking the castled king

Finally we shall look at ways of attacking different pawn formations. Remember that the pawns are there to protect the king; the further they move up the board, the less safe the king becomes.

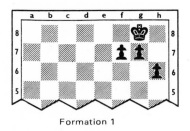

Formation 1

(a) Look for possibility of a bishop sacrifice on h6.

(b) Try to make the black g-pawn move.

(c) Put a knight on f5 to attack g7 and h6.

(d) Consider a pawn attack by g2-g4-g5 to open lines.

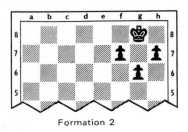

Formation 2

(a) Attack along the diagonals a1-h8 and c1-h6.

(b) Attack the dark squares around the fortress, especially f6 and h6.

(c) Try to remove or exchange Black's dark-squared bishop.

(d) Consider a pawn attack by h2-h4-h5, or f2-f4-f5.

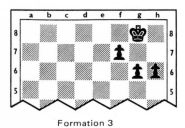

Formation 3

(a) Attack on the dark squares as in Formation 2.

(b) Look for chance of a sacrifice on g6.

(c) Put a bishop on the diagonal a2-g8 to pin the f-pawn and weaken the g-pawn.

(d) Consider a pawn attack with h- or f-pawns, but beware advancing the g-pawn since g4-g5 can be met with . . . h6-h5.

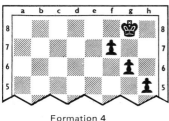

Formation 4

(a) Attack on the dark squares as in Formation 2 and 3.

(b) Look for possibility of a piece sacrifice on g6 or h5.

(c) Put a bishop on the diagonal a2-g8 to pin the f-pawn and weaken the g-pawn.

(d) Consider a pawn attack with g2-g4.

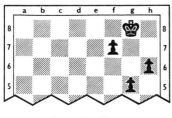

Formation 5

(a) Attack on the diagonals a1-h8 and b1-h7.

(b) Look for possibility of a piece sacrifice on g5.

(c) Try to get your queen or a knight onto h5.

(d) Consider a pawn attack with h2-h4.

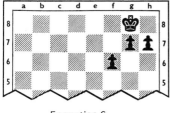

Formation 6

(a) Try to check on the diagonal a2-g8 to force the king into the corner.

(b) Attack h7, which cannot be defended by a knight from f6.

(c) Put a knight on f5 or h5.

(d) Beware a pawn attack; this will be very slow, and g2-g4-g5 can be answered with . . . f6-f5.

SACRIFICING TO DYNAMITE THE CASTLE WALLS

The idea of sacrificing pieces to rip away the pawn shield in front of the enemy king was studied in Chapter 2 (see pages 5–29), and we have seen examples in the last few games. Let us look at one more dramatic reminder here.

Game 48

(Bird's Opening)

1	f2-f4	d7-d5
2	e2-e3	Ng8-f6
3	b2-b3	e7-e6
4	Bc1-b2	Bf8-e7
5	Bf1-d3	b7-b6
6	Nb1-c3	Bc8-b7
7	Ng1-f3	c7-c5
8	0-0	0-0
9	Nc3-e2	

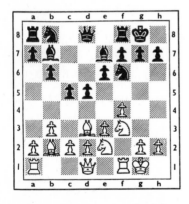

Since the rival centre pawns have not come into contact, there are no open files, and White is not ready to commit his rooks. He realizes that Black will not be able to make headway in the centre, and begins to build up for a K-side attack with his minor pieces.

9	. . .	Nb8-c6
10	Nf3-e5	Nc6xe5
11	Bb2xe5	Qd8-d7
12	Ne2-g3	b6-b5

Black grabs space on the Q-side and threatens 13 . . . c5-c4, pushing back White's light-squared bishop.

13	Ng3-h5	Nf6xh5

If 13 . . . c5-c4 14 Nh5xf6+ Be7xf6 15 Bd3xh7+ Kg8xh7 16 Qd1-h5+ Kh7-g8 17 Be5xf6 g7xf6 18 Qh5-g4+ Kg8-h8 19 Rf1-f3 and Black cannot prevent Rf3-h3 mate.

14	Bd3xh7+!

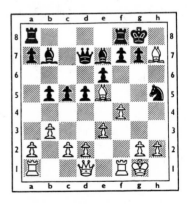

The light-squared bishop is given up to remove one sentry from the fortress wall.

14	. . .	Kg8xh7
15	Qd1xh5+	Kh7-g8
16	Be5xg7!	

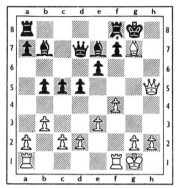

Black has beaten off the immediate mate threat at the cost of his queen, but his king remains horribly exposed, and White is quick to follow up the attack.

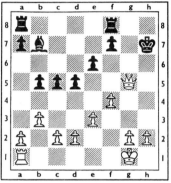

The dark-squared bishop is sacrificed for a second sentry pawn. Black must accept, because mate is threatened by Qh5-h8.

16	. . .	Kg8xg7
17	Qh5-g4+	Kg7-h7

White has wiped out the black sentries and the black king is looking decidedly lonely!

18 Rf1-f3

The white rook isn't just coming to keep the black king company — he's threatening mate!

18	. . .	Qd7-d8
19	Rf3-h3+	Be7-h4
20	Rh3xh4+	Qd8xh4
21	Qg4xh4+	Kh7-g7
22	Qh4-g5+	Kg7-h7

23	Ra1-f1	Rf8-g8
24	Qg5-h5+	Kh7-g7
25	f4-f5	e6-e5

Black cannot let the white rook loose down the f-file.

26	f5-f6+	Kg7-f8

The black king takes refuge behind his last sentry pawn, but White is not long in winkling him out.

27 Qh5xe5

Threatening mate on e7.

27	. . .	Rg8-h8
28	Qe5-e7+	Kf8-g8
29	Rf1-f3	Rh8-h6
30	Rf3-g3+	Rh6-g6
31	Rg3xg6+	f7xg6
32	Qe7-g7 mate	

White sacrificed two minor pieces to dynamite the black fortress, and the black king was left with nowhere to hide and nowhere to run. Even after the sacrifice of his queen, Black found the White attack still grinding relentlessly on.

Sacrificing to rip the fortress walls apart is a fairly obvious way of getting at the enemy king. There are many different ways of sacrificing to destroy the defences, but one particular sacrifice is worth learning, since it occurs quite frequently.

GRECO'S SACRIFICE

The best defensive piece for the K-side is the king's knight.

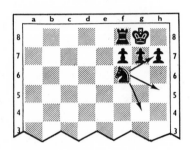

On f6 the black knight does two valuable jobs:

(a) It defends h7.

(b) It stops the white queen from coming to g4 or h5.

The idea of Greco's sacrifice is to take advantage of the absence of the knight from f6; give up a bishop on h7, and continue with a decisive queen-and-knight attack. History tells us that Greco was White in the following game, in 1619:

Game 49

(Irregular Defence)

1	e2-e4	e7-e6
2	d2-d4	Ng8-f6
3	Bf1-d3	Nb8-c6
4	Ng1-f3	Bf8-e7
5	h2-h4	

In 1619 they didn't seem to know much about the openings!

5	...	0-0

6 e4-e5

But Greco was well aware of how useful it can be to drive the defensive knight from f6.

6	...	Nf6-d5

7 Bd3xh7+!

The black king, with only the sentry pawns in front of him, is opened up to the full fury of White's pieces.

7	...	Kg8xh7

If Black doesn't capture the bishop,

then he is just a pawn down and has a hole in his front door.

8   Nf3-g5+

8   ...   Kh7-g8

Black had four other possibilities:
(a) 8 . . . Kh7-h6 9 Ng5xf7++
costs him his queen, while
(b) 8 . . . Kh7-g6 9 h4-h5+ Kg6-f5
10 g2-g4, (c) 8 . . . Kg8-h8 9 Qd1-
h5+ Kh8-g8 10 Qh5-h7, and
(d) 8 . . . Be7xg5 9 h4xg5+ Kh7-g6
10 Qd1-h5+ Kg6-f5 11 Qh5-h3+

Kf5-g6 12 Qh3-h7, are all mate.

9   Qd1-h5   Be7xg5

If 9 . . . Rf8-e8 10 Qh5-h7+
Kg8-f8 11 Qh7-h8 mate.

10   h4xg5   f7-f5

Moving the f-pawn is the only way of meeting both the mate threats, on h7 and h8.

11   g5-g6   Black resigns

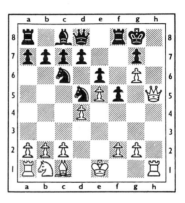

Black cannot now prevent Qh5-h8 mate.

Game 49 showed the basic idea behind Greco's sacrifice, but normally both sides will have castled and the h-pawn won't be able to join the battle. There are then four general conditions for the attack. Assuming White is sacrificing:

(a) The black knight must be missing from f6.

(b) The white knight must be able to go to g5 without danger.

(c) The white queen must be able to come immediately to the light squares on the K-side.

(d) White must have enough attackers in play to catch the king if he comes out into the open.

Game 50 is a more common example of Greco's sacrifice.

Game 50

(Sicilian Defence)

1	e2-e4	c7-c5
2	c2-c3	Ng8-f6
3	e4-e5	Nf6-d5
4	d2-d4	c5xd4
5	c3xd4	d7-d6
6	Ng1-f3	Nb8-c6
7	Nb1-c3	Nd5xc3
8	b2xc3	e7-e6
9	e5xd6	Bf8xd6
10	Bf1-d3	Qd8-a5

11 0-0

White offers a pawn to speed up his development.

11 . . .   Qa5xc3

12 Ra1-b1   0-0?

Black cannot afford to play 12 . . . Nc6xd4 13 Nf3xd4 Qc3xd4 14 Bd3-b5+ because he would lose his queen; however, he doesn't realize quite how much danger there is on the K-side.

13 Rb1-b3   Qc3-a5

All the conditions for Greco's sacrifice are right: (a) the black knight is missing from f6, (b) the white knight will be safe on g5, (c) g4 and h5 are clear for the white queen, and (d) the bishop on c1 and rook on b3 are ready to support the attack.

14 Bd3xh7+!   Kg8xh7

15 Nf3-g5+   Kh7-g6

If the king goes to h8 or g8 then Qd1-h5 forces mate, and if 15 . . . Kg8-h6, the supporting rook joins battle with check on h3.

16 Rb3-h3   Bc8-d7

17 Ng5-e4

Threatening 18 Qd1-g4+.

17 . . .   f7-f6

18 Ne4xd6

White has regained his piece, the black king is out in front of his remaining sentries, and 19 Qd1-g4+ is threatened.

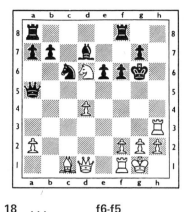

18 ...   f6-f5

19   Qd1-h5+   Kg6-f6

20   Bc1-g5 mate

A sacrifice to demolish the enemy pawn shield should always be in your mind. A piece or two are of no importance if you can lay bare the enemy king and mate him. But, as we learnt in Chapter 2, before you sacrifice you must be absolutely certain that you are going to get somewhere. If you fail to mate the king, and if you cannot win your piece back, then you are in trouble. Sacrifice, smash the enemy defences, rip open his king but, be careful!

SUMMARY

In most games both players will castle on the king's side. You must not even consider beginning to attack your opponent's king until you have a firm hold on the centre of the board. When your pieces do hold the centre you can begin to switch them to the K-side for the attack on the enemy fortress. Even so, you must always keep a watchful eye upon the centre; if your opponent is allowed to counter-attack down the middle, then your pieces will be caught stranded on the wing.

When the centre of the board is blocked, or when you have such massive control that there is no earthly way your opponent can counter-attack, then you can consider throwing your pawns at the enemy. But normally a pawn storm will be too slow, and your pieces will have to do the bulk of the attacking. Then there are two ideas for you to follow: try to weaken the enemy fortress by making the pawn shield advance, and try to obliterate the defensive wall completely by means of a sacrifice.

9 Storming the fortress – castling on opposite wings

When the two players castle on opposite sides of the board—one on the king's wing and the other on the queen's wing—you can generally expect a violent cut-throat battle. Both players storm the fortress, hurling their armies at the enemy king, and they are helped by the fact that their own kings do not get in the way of the attacking pieces. Like two fighters slugging it out in the middle of the boxing ring, the players hack away at each other, until one of them collapses under the onslaught. Look at Game 51

Game 51

(Sicilian Defence—Dragon Variation)

1	e2-e4	c7-c5
2	Ng1-f3	d7-d6
3	d2-d4	c5xd4
4	Nf3xd4	Ng8-f6
5	Nb1-c3	g7-g6
6	Bc1-e3	Bf8-g7
7	f2-f3	0-0
8	Bf1-c4	Nb8-c6
9	Qd1-d2	Bc8-d7
10	0-0-0	

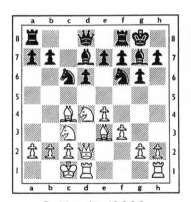

Position after 10 0-0-0

The kings are castled on opposite wings and the stage is set.

The advantage of castling Q-side is that the rook comes straight into action in the centre. The disadvantage is that the king does not defend his fortress properly; the squares a1 and a2 are beyond his reach. However, when you castle K-side, it usually costs you another move getting your rook into play on e1 or d1. So, when you castle Q-side you should be prepared to spend another move on properly defending your fortress, by playing Kc1-b1. This may seem to 'waste' a move which could be used to attack on the other side of the board, but you must balance all-out attack with sensible defence. Your king is the strongest defender of your fortress; if you leave him on c1, you are taking a risk.

10	. . .	Ra8-c8
11	Bc4-b3	Nc6-e5
12	h2-h4	

White fires the first shot!

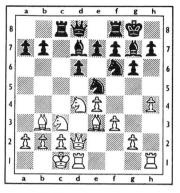

Position after 12 h2-h4

White needs open lines for his pieces, and he must get them quickly. Black obviously plans to counter-attack on the Q-side. The game will turn into a race, and the winner will be the player who gets his attack in first. Normally pawn attacks are slow and risky when the centre isn't blocked. Here however the king's are on opposite wings. Advancing the h-pawn is safe because the K-side pawns are not needed to shield the white king, and quick because there is a weakness in Black's pawn shield. The black pawn on g6 is a target; as soon as White can play h4-h5 he will force open the h-file and his rook will surge into action.

12	. . .	Qd8-a5

Why doesn't Black counter-attack with a pawn storm? When you attack the enemy king position with pawns you are after two things:

(a) You try to exchange pawns and open up the king.

(b) You open lines for your own pieces.

White's pawn advance on the K-side is quick because Black has moved one of his own sentry pawns. A Black pawn storm on the Q-side would be slower because White's sentries are unmoved, and it would take longer for the black pawns to get to grips with them. Clearly, in a pawn storm, Black would lose the race. More important, however, Black doesn't need a pawn storm because he already has the c-file open for his rooks, and can begin a piece attack.

13	h4-h5	

The race is hotting up, and the attack must proceed at top speed. An open file for his rook is worth more to White than his h-pawn.

13	. . .	Nf6xh5
14	Be3-h6	Bg7xh6
15	Qd2xh6	

White looks to be winning easily; his fire-power on the h-file is most impressive, and as we shall see he has a straightforward mating plan.

What can Black do? He has hardly got started on the Q-side, and there are no weaknesses in the White fortress for him to attack.

15 ...   **Rc8xc3!**

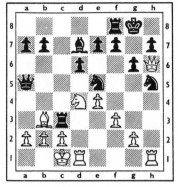

Position after 15 ... Rc8xc3

There are no weaknesses in White's pawn shield, so Black has to make some. White's attack on the K-side is moving quickly, he has terrific firepower on the h-file. There is no point in Black simply trying to defend his king, or quietly continuing to build up a Q-side attack; he doesn't have the time. Black must strike quickly and strike hard; he must give White something to think about, something to take his mind off his own attack.

16 b2xc3

At the expense of the exchange, Black has shattered White's pawn shield.

16 ...   **Rf8-c8**

17 g2-g4   **Nh5-f6**

The knight must defend h7 at all costs.

18 g4-g5   **Nf6-h5**

19 Rh1xh5

White must press on rapidly with the attack, for Black is beginning to look menacing on the Q-side. The knight on h5 is the key to Black's defensive position, so it is dynamited.

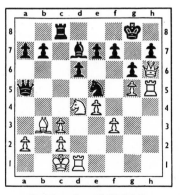

Position after 19 Rh1xh5

19	**...**	**g6xh5**

20	**Qh6xh5**

The first step of White's mating plan is over; he has removed the black knight and cleared the h-file. Now all that remains is for White to play Rd1-h1, capture with his queen on h7, and invite the black king to wave the white flag!

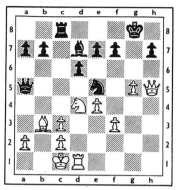

Position after 20 Qh6xh5

20	**...**	**Qa5xc3**

A blow to White's hopes; if 21 Rd1-h1 Ne5-d3+. Now White is beginning to wish he'd found time to play Kc1-b1 earlier.

21	**Kc1-b1**	**Ne5-c4**

Threatening 22 . . . Qc3-b2 mate. Perhaps White isn't winning after all!

22	**Bb3xc4**	**Rc8xc4**

23	**Rd1-d3**

The black queen displays her excellent defensive powers; if 23 Rd1-h1 Qc3xd4 24 Qh5xh7+ Kg8-f8, and she can skip back to defend any threat to her king. White therefore is forced to abandon his attack, and tries to defend himself.

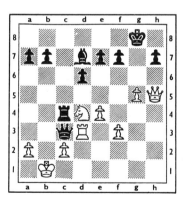

The race is over.

When the kings have castled on opposite wings, victory will usually go to the player who can force his opponent onto the defensive. This is certainly the case here; White is finished off rapidly.

23	. . .	Qc3-e1+
24	Kb1-b2	Qe1-f2

Black renews his threat to the white knight, and also keeps c2 firmly under the microscope.

Position after 24 . . . Qe1-f2

25 g5-g6

White's chief problem has been that whereas the black queen has commanded the centre, tying the white rook to defending the knight, the white queen has done absolutely nothing but support the attack on the h-file. The attack is now dead and the queen is left off-side; she tries to get back into the centre but it is too late.

25	. . .	h7xg6
26	Qh5-d5	Bd7-e6
27	Nd4xe6	

This gets White mated; but 27 Qd5xb7 Rc4xd4 28 Rd3xd4 Qf2xd4 would leave him helpless, a piece and pawn down in the end-game.

27	. . .	Qf2xc2+
28	Kb2-a3	

Or 28 Kb2-a1 Qc2-c1 mate.

| 28 | . . . | Rc4-a4 mate |

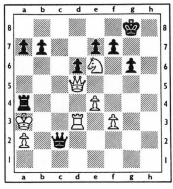

Final position

A race from start to finish, with Black just getting his nose in front on the line. There are five points to remember when playing opposite-wing-castled positions, and this game highlights them all.

(1) Speed is important.

(2) Command of the centre is the springboard for victory.

(3) Piece attacks are quicker than pawn attacks.

(4) Scattered pieces and a weakened fortress speed up a pawn storm.

(5) The pieces must be able to follow up a pawn storm quickly.

SPEED IS IMPORTANT

You must attack, and you must attack quickly. There is no point in sitting back just trying to defend yourself. The attacker will gain space on the side of the board where he is attacking, and this will increase his fire-power. Once this happens, you will be squashed flat. Your only chance is to get a counter-attack going on the other wing or in the centre; give your opponent something else to think about; slow him down a bit.

Of course, you must not throw everything into attack and forget about defence. You must always be on the look-out for a defensive move which makes your king position safer, which holds up the enemy attack. The rule is: *concentrate on attack and only make those defensive moves that are absolutely necessary.* Avoid at all costs being forced to defend. Victory after opposite-wing castling will go to the player who forces his opponent onto the defensive.

COMMAND OF THE CENTRE IS THE SPRINGBOARD FOR VICTORY

Why did Black win Game 51? Why did he win the race of attack?
The moment of truth came for White on move 21

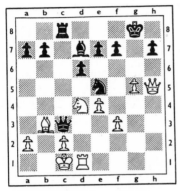

Position after 20 ... Qa5xc3

White's attack has reached its climax,
but he can't carry out his plan to
play 21 Rd1-h1 and finish Black off
along the h-file.

Why not?

Because when the white rook deserts
the d-file the black queen seizes the
centre of the board:

21	Rd1-h1	Ne5-d3+

22	Kc1-d1	

Not 22 Kc1-b1 Qc3-b2 mate.

22	...	Nd3-f2+

23	Kd1-c1	

If 23 Kd1-e2 Nf2xh1 (threatening
24 ... Nh1-g3+) 24 Qh5xf7+

Kg8-f8 25 Qf7xe7 Qc3xd4, and
the black queen covers the threat
of 26 Qe7-f6 mate.

23	...	Nf2xh1
24	Bb3xf7+	Kg8-h8
25	g5-g6	Qc3-a1+
26	Kc1-d2	Qa1xd4+

The black queen dominates the
centre, and White's attack is at an
end. We have seen before the
strength of pieces in the centre;
this is another excellent example.

27	Kd2-c1	Qd4-g7

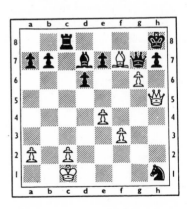

From the centre of the board the black queen can breathe fire in all directions. Here, she shows her defensive powers by beating off White's threat
of 28 Qh5xh7 mate. White can resign; he is a rook and a knight down, and
he can't even play 28 Qh5xh1 because the black queen can then swing into
attack with 28 ... Qg7-a1+!

When kings are castled on opposite wings, look for the chance to attack in the centre; this may be the shortest route to the enemy king. Look at Game 52.

Game 52

(*Queen's Gambit Declined*)

1	d2-d4	d7-d5
2	c2-c4	e7-e6
3	Ng1-f3	Ng8-f6
4	Bc1-g5	Bf8-e7
5	Nb1-c3	Nb8-d7
6	e2-e3	0-0
7	Qd1-c2	Rf8-e8
8	0-0-0	

K-side; Black must quickly begin action on the queen's wing.

11 ...   **d5xc4**

12 Bd3xc4   **c6-c5**

Black desperately tries to open lines on the Q-side for his cramped pieces, but he gives White the chance to attack in the centre.

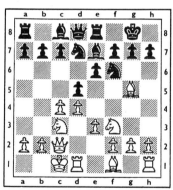

8 ...   **c7-c6**

9 Kc1-b1!

Very sensibly White decides that before making any attacking moves, he will make his king position safer.

9 ...   **Nd7-f8**

Black is already rather cramped.

10 Bf1-d3   **Qd8-a5**

11 h2-h4

White begins a pawn storm on the

13 d4-d5!

After just one move, White's pawn storm on the K-side is postponed. Attack in the centre is far more important, and the white pieces soon take up powerful posts.

13	...	e6xd5
14	Nc3xd5	Nf6xd5
15	Bc4xd5	Bc8-e6
16	Bd5xe6	Nf8xe6
17	Rd1-d7	

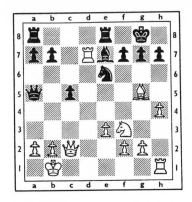

Black has been cut in two straight down the middle; his K-side pieces can't get into the attack, and his Q-side pieces can't help defend their king. White's rook and queen, on the central files, are able to support an attack on the black king while standing ready to fend off a black invasion on the Q-side.

17 ...   Be7-f8

Black had to do something about his bishop, and he could hardly play 17 . . . Be7xg5 18 h4xg5, and let the white rook loose down the h-file.

18 Qc2-f5   Qa5-a4

Black can't hold f7, so he looks for a counter-attack. But what has he got to attack with?

19 Nf3-e5

The black f-pawn isn't going anywhere—19 . . . f7-f6 20 Bg5xf6 g7xf6 21 Qf5xh7 mate—so White is in no hurry to capture. The knight adds its fire-power to the attack, and the white pieces, swing from the centre and quickly surround the black king.

19 ...   b7-b6

20 Qf5xf7+   Kg8-h8

21 f2-f3!

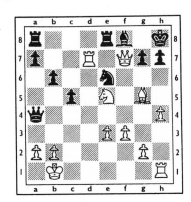

White takes time off from the attack for a simple defensive move. The black queen was threatening to get into the centre with a check on e4, so White denies her this chance.

21 ...   c5-c4

Black tries to throw his pawns forward and open lines, but there are no weaknesses in the white pawn shield, so the pawn storm is far too slow.

22 h4-h5

After one sensible defensive move, White presses on with the attack.

22 ...   c4-c3

23 Ne5-g6+!

White's rook has spent a dozen moves straining at the leash on the h-file; now his chance comes.

23	...	h7xg6
24	h5xg6+	Black resigns

After 24 ... Qa4-h4, 25 Rh1xh4 is
mate.

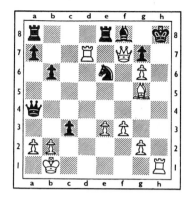

Control of the centre is important in every position; opposite-wing castling
is no exception. If you can control the centre your pieces will be able to
switch easily, one way to attack the enemy king, the other way to defend
your own. Your opponent's army will be cut in two; his defenders and his
attackers won't be able to help each other.

PIECE ATTACKS ARE QUICKER THAN PAWN ATTACKS

Pieces are more powerful than pawns: they move faster, and make nastier
threats. Pawns can march up the board and exchange themselves for the
enemy sentries, opening up the king position. Pawns can march up the
board and force the enemy to weaken his pawn shield by advancing one of
the sentries. Yes, pawns can be useful attackers, but pieces can do the same
job. A piece can destroy the pawn shield by sacrificing itself; a piece can
force an enemy sentry to advance to beat off a threat. *And*, a piece does
not have to march three moves up the board to do it!

Game 53

(King's Gambit—
   Falkbeer Counter Gambit)

1	e2-e4	e7-e5
2	f2-f4	d7-d5
3	e4xd5	e5-d4
4	Bf1-b5+	c7-c6
5	d5xc6	Nb8xc6
6	Nb1-c3	Ng8-f6
7	Qd1-e2	

White is trying to win the black
e-pawn. If he isn't careful his king
will be caught in the centre.

7 ...   **Bf8-c5**

Black quickly clears the way for
castling. At the same time he hits
g1 and makes it impossible for White
to castle K-side.

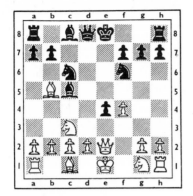

8	Nc3xe4	0-0
9	Bb5xc6	b7xc6
10	d2-d3	Rf8-e8

Life is becoming rather difficult for White along the e-file!

11	Bc1-d2	Nf6xe4
12	d3xe4	Bc8-f5
13	e4-e5	Qd8-b6

Threatening both g1 and b2.

14 0-0-0

Clearly the white king wasn't safe in the centre.

He isn't safe on the Q-side either!

It is already obvious that Black is winning. The kings are on opposite wings, and the game should develop into an attacking race on both sides. However, Black has a definite lead in development, and open lines for his pieces. White is immediately forced onto the defensive. His invasion fleet won't even get time to weigh anchor, let alone set sail.

14 ... Bc5-d4!

In one move Black's bishop forces a weakening of the white pawn shield; ... Qb6xb2 mate is threatened.

15 c2-c3 Ra8-b8!

This forces another weakness in White's pawn shield.

Black could also make White advance his b-pawn by playing ... a7-a5-a4-a3, but this pawn attack takes three moves; the black rook does the job in one.

16 b2-b3 Re8-d8

Black's king's rook makes use of the other open file. White is mated if he dares to capture the bishop: 17 c3xd4 Qb6xd4, threatening 18 ... Qd4-a1.

17 Ng1-f3

Now Black could simply retreat his bishop to c5 and advance his a-pawn to carve open White's king position.

This plan would take at least four moves; the black queen can do the job in one.

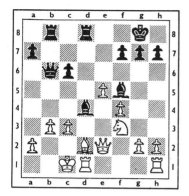

17 ... Qb6xb3!!
Splat! The White pawn shield
crumbles. Mate is threatened on a3,
b1, b2, and c2; so White is forced
to take.

18 a2xb3 Rb8xb3
Threatening mate on b1. White
makes a hole for his king on d2 . . .

19 Bd2-e1 Bd4-e3+
. . . but Black fills it in for him!

20 Qe2xe3 Rh3-b1 mate

When the files and diagonals are open for your pieces to use, get straight
on with a piece attack. The sooner your pieces get into action the sooner
you will make threats, and when you make threats your opponent must
halt his own plans for attack and come and deal with them. The most useful job pawns can do in your attack is to open lines for your pieces. If the
lines are already there, leave the pawns at home.

SCATTERED PIECES AND A WEAKENED FORTRESS SPEED UP A PAWN STORM

The only trouble with a pawn storm is that it is very slow. Given enough
time, your pawns could take any enemy fortress apart, and leave the king
open, awaiting your execution squad. Unfortunately, you don't always
have enough time. Pawn storms are speeded up if:

(a) The enemy pawn shield is weakened by one of the pawns having
advanced, so that your pawn will get to grips with the enemy sooner, and
it will be easier to force open a file.

(b) Enemy pieces are scattered in the path of the advancing pawns, so
that your opponent has to waste time moving them to safety.

This is all fairly obvious, so we shall just look at one simple example.

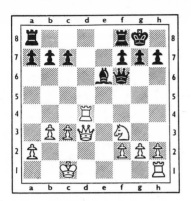

Black to move

The kings stand on opposite wings and both sides are preparing to storm the fortress. Only one minor piece on each side is left; so the rooks must play a major part if either side is to draw up enough fire-power to checkmate his opponent. Rooks need open files; so both sides will throw up their pawns. Who will break through first? If we study the position for a few moments it won't take long to see that Black has the advantage. There are weaknesses in White's pawn shield, and the white pieces in the centre are targets for the black c-pawn. On the K-side Black's pawns stand in a solid line; it will take White a long time to make progress.

| 1 | ... | c7-c5 |

The first step in the black pawn storm, and it comes free of charge. The black c-pawn forces the white rook to move; so White must lose time.

| 2 | Rd4-d6 | a7-a5 |
| 3 | h2-h4 | a5-a4 |

Black is miles ahead already in the race; his pawn storm has made contact with the white sentries, and he threatens 4 . . . a4xb3 5 a2xb3 Ra8-a1+ winning a rook.

| 4 | Kc1-b2 |

The king defends his sentries, but Black soon tears the flimsy shield to shreds.

| 4 | ... | a4xb3 |
| 5 | a2xb3 | c5-c4! |

Again Black gains time; White cannot ignore Black's pawn storm and continue with his own attack, because his queen is threatened.

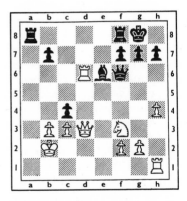

| 6 | b3xc4 |

White would dearly have loved to have been able to block the Q-side by 6 Qd3-d4 Qf6-g6 7 b3-b4 and prevent Black from getting open lines for his pieces, but Black had a brilliant reply: 7 . . . Ra8-a2+! 8 Kb2xa2 Qg6-c2+, and 9 . . . Rf8-a8 mate.

6 ...   b7-b5!

Yet again a black pawn strides forward, strikes immediately at the enemy, and threatens to smash open more lines. There's not a lot left of the white pawn shield! White realizes he can't defend the Q-side and decides to go out fighting.

7   Nf3-g5

Threatening mate on h7. White had nothing better: 7 c4xb5 Ra8-a2+ 8 Kb2-b1 Rf8-a8   9 Rd6-a6 Ra2xa6 10 b5xa6 Be6-f5, costs him his queen, and 7 h4-h5 b5xc4 simply opens the lock gates and allows the black rooks to flood in along the Q-side files.

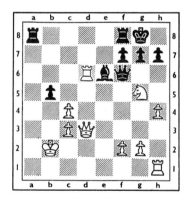

7   ...   Qf6xf2+

8   Qd3-d2

Or (a) 8 Kb2-b1 Be6-f5+, (b) Qd3-

c2 Ra8-a2+, (c) 8 Kb2-b3 Be6xc4+, (d) 8 Kb2-c1 Ra8-a1 mate.

8   ...   Qf2-a7

9   Qd2-d3

White can't prevent the coming invasion along the a-file, so he renews his own mating threat.

9   ...   Qa7-a2+

10   Kb2-c1   g7-g6

White has at last forced a weakness, but ten moves too late.

11   Ng5xe6

What else?

11   ...   Qa2xg2

12   Rh1-d1   Ra8-a1+

13   Qd3-b1   Ra1xb1+

14   Kc1xb1   f7xe6

15   White resigns

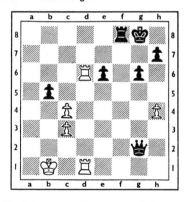

Black has won the race easily!

Black's pawn storm quickly opened files and paved the way for the piece invasion, because as the pawns advanced they were able to gain time by threatening White's pieces, and by getting into immediate battle with the weakened white pawn shield.

THE PIECES MUST BE ABLE TO FOLLOW UP A PAWN STORM QUICKLY

Your pawns may be able to advance and carve great chunks out of the enemy fortress, but this will be of no use at all if your pieces are not placed to follow up the attack, to flood in through the holes and seize the king.

Game 54

(Queen's Gambit Declined—

Slav Defence)

1	d2-d4	d7-d5
2	c2-c4	e7-e6
3	Ng1-f3	Ng8-f6
4	Nb1-c3	c7-c6
5	e2-e3	Bf8-e7
6	Qd1-c2	0-0
7	Bc1-d2	Nb8-d7
8	0-0-0	Rf8-e8

The opening is similar to Game 52, and Black again finds himself rather cramped.

9 e3-e4

White is prepared to risk leaving his king on c1; he presses on immediately to make the most of his advantage in space.

9	. . .	Nd7-f8
10	e4-e5	Nf6-d7

11 h2-h4

The centre is blocked with pawns and there are no open files. A pawn storm is needed to increase the firepower of the white rooks, and White gets straight on with the job. The advance will be slow, since there are no weaknesses in Black's pawn shield, nor any pieces for the white pawns to attack on the way. However, White realizes that Black has not finished his development, is

short of space, and will take some time to work up a counter-attack.

11	. . .	Nd7-b6
12	g2-g4	Nb6xc4
13	Bf1xc4	d5xc4

14 g4-g5

Black has won a pawn, but White has won three important moves, and his pawns stand at the gates of the black fortress.

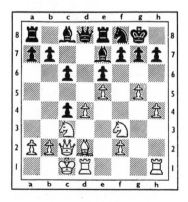

14 . . . b7-b5

The counter-attack is under way.

15 Nc3-e4

Black has several pieces ready to defend his K-side; so the white pawns cannot batter their way in alone. The knight comes to the centre to give them support.

15 ...   b5-b4

16 Ne4-f6+!

The knight is first to knock on Black's door. If now 16 . . . g7xf6 17 g5xf6 and White has trapped the black bishop and opened the g-file for his rooks.

16 ...   Be7xf6

17 g5xf6   b4-b3

Black's pawn storm keeps pace with White's; the race looks neck and neck.

18 a2xb3   c4xb3

19 Qc2-e4

Naturally White doesn't want to take the black b-pawn. As long as the pawn remains on b3 Black has no chance of attacking along the b-file.

19 ...   Bc8-a6

Similarly, Black doesn't worry about 20 f6xg7. The black king would be perfectly safe in front of the white pawn, and White would lose the g-file as a line of attack. After all, he can't take his own pawn!

20 Rd1-g1

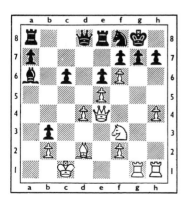

The race may have looked neck and neck, but in fact White is winning easily. Black's pawn storm may have ripped White's line of sentries apart, but his pieces are in no position to take advantage of the weaknesses. The black rooks still haven't got an open file, the black queen can't go to a5, the bishop is pointing the wrong way, and the knight is stuck at home defending. Black has absolutely nothing! On the other hand the white pieces are well placed to support their pawn storm and are already planning to dismantle the black king's position.

20 ...   Nf8-g6

Black has to prevent 21 Rg1xg7+, and 20 . . . g7-g6 won't do because of 21 Qe4-f4, when the white queen wriggles in to mate on g7.

21 h4-h5

Tally ho!

21 ...   Qd8-d5

22 h5xg6!!

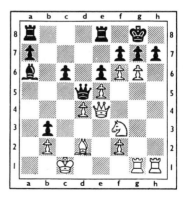

A queen sacrifice! There is no stopping the white pawns now that they have scented blood. With the white pieces snapping at their heels they sink their teeth deep into the black pawn shield.

22 ...   Qd5xe4

23 g6xf7+   Kg8xf7

Black is mated spectacularly after 23 . . . Kg8-h8 by 24 f6xg7! The only other move for Black is equally hopeless: 23 . . . Kg8-f8 24 Bd2-b4+ Kf8xf7 23 Rg1xg7 mate.

24 Nf3-g5+   Kf7-g6

If the black king retreats, White first wins the rook on e8 and then captures the queen: (a) 24 . . . Kf7-g8 25 f6-f7+ Kg8-h8 26 f7xe8=Q+ Ra8xe8 27 Ng5xe4, or (b) 24 . . . Kf7-f8 25 Bd2-b4+ etc., and in both cases White has a large advantage in pieces.

25 Ng5xe4+   Kg6-f5

With 25 . . . Kg6-f7 26 Rg1xg7+ Kf7-f8 27 Bd2-b4+, Black would avoid mate, but would be so far behind on material that he could safely resign!

26 Ne4-d6 mate

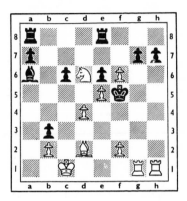

The white pieces have finished off the splendid work done by the pawns. Indeed, if the pieces had not been in a position to follow up the attack, the pawns' work would have been useless. Black's pawns also did a good job, but his pieces were badly placed—they could not support their pawns—and the attack came to an end.

Pawns lack the power of pieces, and they cannot perform miracles. Alone they may destroy the enemy fortress, but they need the help of the main army if checkmate is to be achieved. When you begin a pawn storm make sure your pieces will be able to follow up; if they can't, then no matter how large a dent your pawns may make in the enemy pawn shield, you will simply be wasting your time!

SUMMARY

When the kings have castled on opposite wings, you have two battle-fields; one on which you attack, the other on which you defend. Both sides will have an advantage in space on the side of the board where the enemy king stands. This means that on both battle-fields the attacking forces will have more room to move around, more files and diagonals, than the defenders. Both attacks in fact would probably win; both attacks would muster enough fire-power to smash the enemy defences. However, only one attack *can* win—the attack that breaks through first. After opposite-wing castling, the game is a race between the two attacks.

When you are running a race, speed is all that matters. You have to get from the start to the finish as quickly as possible. Yet if the rules allowed you to stop for a few seconds to place some obstacle in the path of all the other runners, so that they would fall flat on their faces, then those few seconds would be very well spent! On the chess-board, in positions of opposite-wing castling, you must attack, attack, and attack, but look out for the odd defensive move which will slow the opponent down, or even stop his attack dead.

Always remember the most important part of the board is the centre. If you can win the centre after opposite-side castling, you will control both battle-fields, your pieces will be able to switch to one side or the other, to attack or defend, and your opponent will be cut in two down the middle.

Attack with your pieces whenever you can; piece attacks are quicker and carry far more fire-power. If you do not have the open lines for your pieces, then the pawns must advance and clear the way. Look for ways of gaining time with your pawn advance; look for pieces to attack, or weaknesses in the enemy pawn shield. Remember that a pawn attack on its own will be quite useless; your pieces must be able to follow up. Your pawns may rip the holes in the enemy fortress, but your pieces must be able to finish the job of slaying the king.

Opposite-wing-castled games are the most exciting battles on the chess-board. You know now how to attack; before castling on the opposite wing to your opponent, think hard. Think about all the ways of attacking, look for weaknesses in the king position, look to see who has the better attacking lines for the pieces. Remember the game will be a race; castle on the opposite side when you are sure that your opponent won't be knocking at your door first. Storm the fortress, and get there first.

Epilogue

He'd won.

Mr. Woodpusher didn't need to ask or to look at the board; the smug expression of pleasure and self-satisfaction on Bobby's face told him all he wanted to know.

'I won!' Bobby announced proudly.

'Er . . . yes, I rather guessed you had.' Mr. Woodpusher replied. 'Well done.'

'And it was brilliant too,' Bobby rattled on. 'I sacrificed a pawn and a piece, then a rook, then another piece. I absolutely tore his defences to bits, drove his king up the board and mated him! I smashed him, and I was still two pieces down at the end.'

Mr. Woodpusher smiled; he knew only too well what was coming next.

'Brilliant, it was really. Look, I'll show you . . .', Bobby rapidly set up the pieces.

Mr. Woodpusher groaned to himself and sat down.

Game 55
(*Budapest Gambit*)

Bobby Blunder Unfortunate Opponent

1	d2-d4	Ng8-f6
2	c2-c4	e7-e5
3	d4xe5	Nf6-g4
4	e2-e4	

'I thought it would be better to control the centre rather than try to hang on to the pawn.'

4	. . .	Ng4xe5
5	f2-f4	Ne5-g6
6	Ng1-f3	

'You might have done better to play 6 a2-a3, stopping . . . Bf8-b4+.' Mr. Woodpusher interrupted. 'But your move develops a piece, so it can't be too bad . . .'

Bobby wasn't listening; he had already played the next move.

6	. . .	Bf8-b4+
7	Bc1-d2	

'That's a really awful move.' Mr. Woodpusher said calmly.

Bobby looked up startled. 'No it's not! . . . Anyway, what should I have done?'

'The only good move is 7 Nb1-c3; you don't have to worry about 7 . . . Bd4xc3+ 8 b2xc3 since you get a splendid diagonal for your bishop on a3 in exchange for the doubled pawns.'

Bobby didn't look at all impressed.

'In fact,' Mr. Woodpusher went on, 'your move loses a pawn.'

Now Bobby looked quite disgruntled.

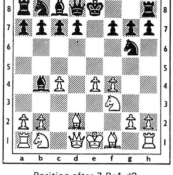

Position after 7 Bc1-d2

7	. . .	Qd8-e7
8	Bf1-d3	Ng6xf4

'See what I mean?' Mr Woodpusher remarked happily. 'You've lost a pawn . . . and you've got a rotten position as well!'

9	0-0	

'That doesn't look a very bright idea either.'

Bobby was beginning to wish he hadn't allowed Mr. Woodpusher the opportunity to look at his masterpiece.

9	. . .	Bb4-c5+
10	Kg1-h1	Nf4xd3
11	Bd2-g5	f7-f6

'I missed that,' Bobby admitted. 'I thought he would have to move his queen somewhere, and then I could take his knight.'

Mr. Woodpusher looked rather surprised by Bobby's honesty.

'Anyway, it doesn't matter,' Bobby went on, 'I can follow it up by giving away a rook, and then I get a tremendous attacking going. It's really quite a brilliant sacrifice!'

'Oh, is it?' Mr. Woodpusher said doubtfully.

12	Bg5xf6	Nd3-f2+
13	Rf1xf2	Qe7xf6
14	Nb1-c3	

'There! Do you see? I've sacrificed the rook to get all the pieces into play.' Bobby sat back proudly. 'The attack really gets going now.'

'Oh, does it?' Mr. Woodpusher said, even more doubtfully.

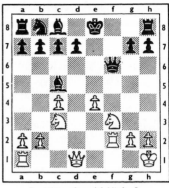

Position after 14 Nb1-c3

14 ...   **Bc5xf2**

15 Nc3-d5

'Now I'm winning!'

'Actually you're losing, but never mind . . . carry on, it's quite interesting.'

15 ...   **Qf6-d6**

'Why didn't he play 15 . . . Qf6-d8? 'Mr. Woodpusher asked. 'Then he's defending c7 and you can't even play Nf3-g5 . . . in fact there's not much you can do, and you are a rook and a piece down. You could always resign, I suppose,' he added brightly.

Bobby decided to ignore that remark.

16 Qd1-e2   **Bf2-b6**

Again Mr. Woodpusher had a question ready. 'Why didn't he just keep up with development with . . . 0-0 or . . . Nb8-c6; he's so far ahead on pieces he can afford to give a bishop back to solve his development problems. And if he *does* get developed, you've got nothing. What can you do?'

'Oh, I would think of something,' Bobby replied cheerfully.

17 e4-e5   **Qd6-c5**

18 Nf3-g5   **0-0**

19 Qe2-h5

'I'm threatening checkmate on h7 now, in case you hadn't noticed.'

Mr. Woodpusher just smiled; he had noticed!

19 ...   **h7-h6**

'That was forced,' Bobby began. 'Now comes the really brilliant bit!'

20 Nd5-f6+

'Great isn't it?' Bobby said, looking up. There was no doubt about it, Mr. Woodpusher was definitely looking more impressed.

20 ...   **Rf8xf6**

'He had to take that way,' Bobby went on. 'If he had captured with the pawn, or if he had moved his king to h8, I would have moved my queen to g6 and mated him next move on h7.'

21 e5xf6

'Now I'm mating him.'

21 ... h6xg5

'Wait a minute, wait a minute,' Mr. Woodpusher interrupted. 'Why couldn't he play 21 ... Qc5xg5? After 22 Qh5-e8+ Kg8-h7 23 f6-f7 Bb6-c5 24 Qe8xc8 Nb8-c6 25 Qc8xa8 Qg5-f6 he's still winning.'

'Yes, but I've got a lot of my pieces back.'

'Perhaps; but you're still losing,' Mr. Woodpusher reminded him. 'Any - way, let's see how you finish him off.

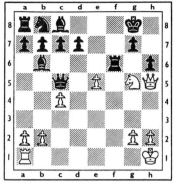

Position after 20 . . . Rf8xf6

22 Qh5-e8+ Kg8-h7

'If he'd put his queen in the way on f8 I would have won her with 23 f6-f7+.

23 Qe8-f7

At last Bobby detected a look of real approval on Mr. Woodpusher's face. Encouraged, he carried on with enthusiasm. 'I'm threatening to mate him on g7, so he has no choice.'

23 ... Kh7-h6

24 f6xg7

'Now I'm threatening g7-g8=N mate!' Mr. Woodpusher looked most amused.

24 ... g5-g4

Mr. Woodpusher's smile broadened . . .

25 g7-g8=N+ Kh6-g5

. . . until the grin split his whole face from ear to ear.

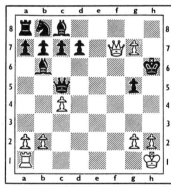

Position after 24 f6xg7

26 Qf7-f6+ Kg5-h5

27 Qf6-h6 mate

'There, I said it was brill . . . Hey! What are you laughing at?'

Mr. Woodpusher looked a little guilty. 'Oh, nothing,' he said. 'I was just remembering another of your games which ended with a pawn reaching the back row and becoming a knight . . . !'

Bobby looked decidedly upset. The game had been superb, and now Mr. Woodpusher was laughing at him. After all he had won, hadn't he? What more did the wretched man want?

'Really you just swindled him, but it was a very entertaining game, and it shows you have remembered something,' Mr. Woodpusher began 'Let's see what else we can learn.'

'The opening you played badly; you lost a pawn on move eight, you threw away a bishop immediately after that, and on move fourteen you gave a rook away for virtually nothing. You were completely lost, and could have resigned by move fifteen.'

If Bobby had looked upset before, his face now registered absolute horror. He had not bargained for this at all.

'Then your opponent played a couple of poor moves and gave you a chance. Fortunately you were fully awake; you seized your opportunity, and began to play really well.'

Bobby began to look a little brighter.

'Mind you, you were still losing; but you played sensibly. When you are losing badly on material it is not always a good idea to play the best moves. What you should do is look for the best chances; look for ways of worrying your opponent and making him go wrong. Look at your position after move 13.

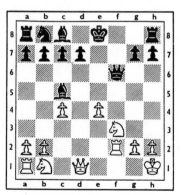

Position after 13 . . . Qe7xf6

'You are a piece behind and you have nothing for it. Here you decided your best plan was to go for an all-out attack on the black king. An excellent idea! After all, what have you got to lose? You are losing anyway, so you can afford to take risks; if you must lose you may as well go out fighting! The moves you played weren't the best, but they attacked your opponent's king; he became worried and he made those all important mistakes that let you off the hook.

'Sometimes it can be fun losing! You have nothing to lose, you can take outrageous risks, and your opponent has to do all the worrying; really you are just trying to swindle him.

'Whenever you fall behind in material always look to see whether you can work up an attack on the enemy king; the king is the natural target for a swindle.'

Bobby nodded. It hadn't really been such a good game after all. 'I was a bit lucky,' he admitted. 'I think he got a bit careless because he was winning so easily.'

'Exactly,' Mr. Woodpusher replied. 'He's sitting there, a rook and a piece ahead, wondering why you don't resign. This is the ideal set up for a swindle; he gets thoroughly fed up and bored, he plays a couple of careless moves, and suddenly he sees you have chances. Then he panics, and begins to think of what he should have done, and how silly he has been; from then on he's fighting himself and his nerves, as well as you. Then he makes the fatal mistake and you've got him!'

'Yes,' said Bobby. 'Because I'm attacking his king, and it doesn't matter what has happened during the game, it is the final position that counts.'

'Correct,' continued Mr. Woodpusher. 'And checkmate ends a game of chess!'

Index of openings

About the Author

J. N. Walker has been chess champion of Oxfordshire several times. He is
a school-teacher, and he runs a junior chess club. He therefore has a thorough
understanding both of the game and of the problems of young players. He
also believes strongly that they should understand principles rather than
memorize examples, and in his books he concentrates on getting the
principles across as clearly and as interestingly as possible.

Another chess book from Oxford

J. N. Walker: **CHESS OPENINGS FOR JUNIORS**

168 pages. Algebraic notation.

A sound understanding of opening principles is the key to effective chess.
Before you launch an attack on the king you must be properly prepared;
you must get your pieces developed on to good squares; you must try to
gain time and space.

In *Chess Openings for Juniors* John Walker explains how to develop the
pieces, and discusses the importance of space and the centre. He surveys
the principal opening systems, and finally suggests how you should set
about choosing your own repertoire, and avoid the disasters which always
seem to happen to Bobby Blunder.

 If you would like to receive regular information about Oxford
Chess Books, we should be happy to send you our free bulletin
twice a year. Just send your name and address on a postcard to:

Oxford University Press (Chess)
Freepost
Oxford OX2 6BR

No stamp is required if you post the card in the United Kingdom.